I, JC

by Charlie Josephine

SAMUEL FRENCH

FOR AMATEUR PRODUCTION ENQUIRIES

UNITED KINGDOM AND WORLD
EXCLUDING NORTH AMERICA
licensing@concordtheatricals.co.uk
020-7054-7298

Each title is subject to availability from Concord Theatricals, depending upon country of performance.

USE OF COPYRIGHTED MUSIC

USE OF COPYRIGHTED THIRD-PARTY MATERIALS

IMPORTANT BILLING AND CREDIT REQUIREMENTS

I, JOAN was first produced by The Globe in August 2022. The performance was directed by Illinca Radulian, and Sarah Dickenson was the dramaturg. Movement direction and choreography by Jennifer Jackson. Set design by Naomi Kuyck-Cohen. Music composed by Laura Moody. Music performed by Joley Cragg, Hannah Dilkes, Hanna Mbuya and Kiyomi Seed. Stage Managers were Felix Dunning, Carol Pestridge and Rachel Middlemore. Assistant Director was Joanna Pidcock. Design Associate was Hazel Low. Costume Supervisor was Laura Rushton. Casting Director was Becky Paris. The production was supported by Gendered Intelligence and All About Trans. The cast was as follows:

JOAN	Isobel Thom
CHARLES / MAURICE	Jolyon Coy
DUNOIS / TOURAINE	Jonah Russell
THOMAS / DELAFONTAINE	Adam Gillen
MARIE / COURCELLES	Janet Etuk
YOLANDE / MANCHON	Debbie Korley
MAN ONE / SOLDIER THREE / BISHOP / BEAUPERE	Kevin McMonagle
MAN THREE / SOLDIER TWO / LOYSELEUR	Esmonde Cole
MAN TWO / SOLDIER ONE / CLERK	Baker Mukasa
JOAN'S ARMY ONE / CAUCHON	Anna Savva
JOAN'S ARMY TWO / GRIS / GIRL	Natasha Cottriall
JOAN'S ARMY THREE	Roseanna Anderson
JOAN'S ARMY FOUR	Joe Henry
JOAN'S ARMY FIVE	Azara Meghie

CHARACTERS

JOAN – They/Them. Seventeen years old. AFAB, nonbinary, working class. Strong and sweet, tender and brave. ADHD is part of their superpower.

CHARLES – He/Him. The Dauphin, then, thanks to Joan, the King of France. Early thirties. Charismatic and powerful. Restless and hungry.

DUNOIS – He/Him. One of many men to overcome. Thirty-plus years old. An excellent soldier. Seasoned veteran. Hard-faced but kind eyes. Written in a northern accent, just cus it felt right.

THOMAS – He/Him. Joan's only possible friend. Working class. Mid-twenties. Intelligent, charming, eager to please.

MARIE – She/Her. Queen of France, but never crowned. Charles' wife. Mid-twenties. Lieutenant of the king with power of attorney. Feminine and powerful. Heavily pregnant.

YOLANDE – She/Her. Duchess of Anjou and Countess of Provence. Finances all operations. Fearsome, gorgeous, powerful. Mid-forties. Marie's mother.

MAN ONE – He/Him. One of Charles' courtiers. A stalwart, and stubborn, he served Charles' father.

MAN TWO – He/Him. One of Charles' courtiers. Aristocratic, charming, a tactician.

MAN THREE – He/Him. One of Charles' courtiers. A junior, eager to learn, keen for action.

DANCER ONE – She/Her. A widow, numb, and needing a spark of inspiration.

DANCER TWO – She/Her. A young woman, unhappily married, praying for hope.

CAUCHON, DELAFONTAINE, GRIS, TOURAINE, MANCHON, LOYSELEUR, COURCELLES, BEAUPERE, CLERK – The men who put Joan on trial. All doctors, masters and bishops. Some could be played by Joan's Army in Act II.

JOAN'S ARMY – She/They/He. Dancers, untrained but confident in their bodies. Sometimes referred to as 'Dancer' when speaking. AFAB, young, queer and fierce as fuck.

Also there's lots of Soldiers and Men at court. Usually numbered to help delineate between actors. Some could be played by Joan's Army in Act II.

AUTHOR'S NOTES

/ indicates a fast run onto the next line, almost an interruption.

/.. indicates where a word can't be found, and the actor does something physical to express themself. It could be a small, pedestrian gesture or a big, abstract movement.

. on its own line indicates where a character should have a line, but is choosing not to speak.

All the actors multi-role, except the actor playing Joan.

THANK YOUS

Thank you to Sean Holmes, Ilinca Radulian, Michelle Terry and Jessica Lusk for believing in me enough to give me this gig. Thank you Sarah Dickenson, brilliant dramaturg, for your fizzy brain and your big heart. Thank you Morgan Llyod Malcolm for always holding the door open behind you. Thank you Dr Will Tosh for your queer history knowledge and guidance. Thank you Jonathan at The Agency for your care and patience and humour. Thank you to Gendered Intelligence and All About Trans for your collaboration and support. Enormous personal thanks to Trans Plus, Spectra, Exceptional Individuals and NHS England for helping me blossom this summer. Thank you Mum for your fierce love. Thank you beautiful Jessica for yours. Thank you to all the queer elders for showing me the way, and to all the beauitful bois for being my fuel.

PROLOGUE

*(**JOAN** climbs up onto the big, empty stage. They look at us, taking everyone in. They smile.)*

JOAN. Trans people are sacred. We are the divine. We are practising our divinity by expressing authenticity. By enjoying our multiplicity. Elevating our humanity, finding the unity hidden inside community, remembering our collective connectivity fuels courageous creativity, unlocking the blessed spiritually that we all seek, yeah, this shit's about to get spiritual. Setting aside all religiosity, we'll focus instead on more of a, street God, if you will. A God for the queers, and the drunks, and the beautiful fuck-ups. A God for the Godless. A God for you, if you want, tonight. Because tonight? Is a celebration. Is a holy communion, for saints and sinners and everyone in between. We offer you restitution. We offer you revolution. We offer you love. I am here, to share my story, to receive God, and to offer you love.

And yeah, I'm fucking frightened. I'm seventeen! But I have a job to do that's bigger than me. You see, I was born into a world on fire, a world at war. The men have been fighting for eighty years or more. I mean, *eighty, years*, and still nowhere near peace?! An insignificant life was my destiny, small, quiet. A nobody from nowhere, a poor farm girl with nothing but a list of duties and expectations. Work hard, marry a man, bear children, die quietly. I always suspected, secretly, that I might be destined for more, but I hardly dared hope. Then suddenly? A miracle occurred! Some unexpected divinity, a moment of love, pure, deep Love! Zzzwoam!

Sudden alignment with Creativity herself, and I'm blessed with a calling, with a purpose far greater than my mind can hold alone. Clarity and confidence like I've never known. God lit a fire in my belly and I'm burning, I am burning, I am *burning* with possibility! I have a vision of Infinite Grace! Of Limitless Expansion! Of Delicious Fluid Freedom, of Liberation, of Joy! And I pray we *all* have the courage to be open to the Infinite, because none of us fit these man-made boxes, none of us fit them at all!

I mean, it's an *honour* to be a human! It's a *beautiful* thing!

So yeah, I'm scared, but really I'm honoured to be here. I honour all who came before, who made it *possible* for *me* to be *here*. So for them, and for me and for you, I'll be brave.

Because my story has been told a thousand different times, a thousand different ways, by everyone but me. Men have told my story, of course. They've grabbed the pen and made it their own as men are want to do. You see, men write stories, about men, for other men. Call them examinations of mankind. Meaning examinations of man. Forget to be kind, forgetting that their kind isn't the only point of view, that there's other ways to see, to be. Yeah, men have written about me, a lot. And most of the words they chose were wrong. It's embarrassing really, how much they've all missed the point. The erasure is pure violence of course, but also, honestly? It's fucking embarrassing.

Truth is, queerness is magic, pure magic! We are beautiful, and powerful, and for that we are killed. The violence is real. We all know how my story ends. So yeah, thank you, for letting me grab this beginning moment here with you. Thank you for being here. Thank you for kindness, for giving me courage.

I am Joan. This is my story. This is my Truth. And this, is my band.

> *(Loud music. The world spins. Musicians and* **MEN** *flood the stage.* **JOAN** *disappears.)*

ACT I

Scene One

(The music and the MEN settle into stillness and silence. 1428, Chinon, France. Stuck inside with nothing to do. The boredom is unbearable.)

CHARLES. Oh god I'm bored!

(The MEN are shocked but try to hide it.)

I said I'm *bored*! ...Oh! Why is life so dull? ...Thomas?

THOMAS. Yes sir?

CHARLES. Why is life so dull?

THOMAS. I, I don't know sir.

CHARLES. Oh God you're boring too! This is all *so boring*! So boring it's almost interesting! How is that possible? As if it loops back on itself?!

(The MEN sneak looks at each other. CHARLES groans.)

Boring boring Boring Boring BORING! Ugh! So bored am I, that it's become appealing to consider chewing my own arm off! At the very least for something to do! Something to feel!

MAN ONE. *(Impatient.)* Sir!

CHARLES. What?

MAN ONE. Forgive me, sir but we are, *at war*!

CHARLES. I know! And who knew that being at war was so dull?! Can't we go and, fight, someone, anyone?!

MAN TWO. We have limited resources sir /

CHARLES. I know!

MAN TWO. The English have fresh reinforcements!

MAN ONE. Nearly three thousand men /

MAN TWO. Which brings their number to a total strength of possibly /

MAN ONE. Ten thousand or more!

CHARLES. I know! I know I know I know! I have been informed. And the repetition is terribly dull... Can't we at least leave this place? Even the name of it is ugly. Chinon. Chinon. *Chinon.* Chin /

MAN ONE. Sir! Please, focus!

CHARLES. Focus on what? Give me something to focus on! Please, I beg you!

MAN ONE. Sir! You are the Dauphin!

CHARLES. Yes! Though God only knows why.

MAN TWO. You are *chosen*! You have a Great Responsibility to lead the Good people of France /

CHARLES. Lead them where? There is nowhere to lead them! The situation is hopeless!

MAN TWO. Sir, please! Keep the faith!

CHARLES. What faith? *What, faith?!*

MAN TWO. Sir! I must say I am shocked!

MAN ONE. Yes, as am I! We can all see what Great burden you carry sir /

MAN TWO. But you *must* make a decision!

MAN ONE. Yes, and quickly! We've been waiting here for *months* now, whilst the English are advancing /

MAN TWO. And our people are dying /

CHARLES. Yes, yes!

MAN ONE. We've offered you many solutions sir, and you've yet to make a decision.

MAN TWO. What are our orders?!

CHARLES. I /.. I /..

> (**CHARLES** *doesn't know. The* **MEN** *look to each other, horrified and frustrated.*)

Thomas?

MAN ONE. Sir! Might *I* suggest, as I have, *many* times before now, that we /

MAN TWO. Withdraw to the East!

MAN ONE. Excuse me /

MAN TWO. As *I* have suggested, over and over /

MAN ONE. No /

MAN TWO. For *months* now! Withdraw to the East and re-group /

MAN ONE. No, no sir /

MAN TWO. Which will strengthen our position in the South!

MAN ONE. Sir, I speak now, with *all* my years of experience! The time has come, we *must* consider a treaty!

MAN TWO. Treaty?! Traitor!

MAN ONE. How dare you?!

MAN TWO. We shall *never* sign a treaty with our enemy!

MAN ONE. I have been at court longer than you have been alive!

MAN TWO. Exactly! Stale old man!

MAN ONE. Ex-*cuse* me?!

CHARLES. Oh please! Quit squabbling! It's terribly dull.

MAN TWO. Sir, sir I promise you /

MAN ONE. Sir, I served your father! And I can assure you, he would never, *never* /

CHARLES. *(Suddenly serious.)* Do not speak of him. Do not, speak of him.

MAN ONE. *(Apologetic.)* Sir, forgive me! I spoke out of /

CHARLES. You know not what you speak of. So your every word fails to capture the truth of it, fails to even come close.

MAN ONE. Yes sir. I'm sorry sir /

CHARLES. My father was a mad man. His madness more terrifying than you'll ever know. He truly believed he was made of glass. Did you know that? Feared he would shatter if he were touched.

MAN ONE. I, I heard rumours as such /

CHARLES. The rumours aren't nearly wild enough, believe me. /.. The things I've seen? /.. And then my mother? My, *mother*! If you can call her that. She /.. Thomas!

THOMAS. Sir.

> *(**THOMAS** rushes over to **CHARLES**. **CHARLES** holds him tight and strokes his hair. The other **MEN** can't look at them, or can't look away.)*

CHARLES. She cast me out! Into the streets Thomas!

THOMAS. Yes sir.

CHARLES. Like a peasant boy! Running through Paris all night in my pyjamas?! Oh the shame, the shame!

(**CHARLES** *squeezes* **THOMAS** *tight, genuinely scared. Then pushes him away and neatens himself.* **MAN ONE** *and* **TWO** *stare, horrified.*)

But come, gentlemen! What's done is done! He chose his son-in-law over his true son, and she abandoned me. So I am disinherited. *Illegitimate.* Oh what a cruel word that is. *Illegitimate!*

MAN ONE. Sir, please, do not speak this way!

CHARLES. Why not? It is the truth, I am rejected!

MAN ONE. No!

CHARLES. Ridiculed!

MAN ONE. Nonsense!

MAN TWO. The people love you!

CHARLES. They *laugh* at me!

MAN TWO. No sir!

CHARLES. I am the laughing stock of France. Ugh! I should be King! Thomas? I should be King?!

THOMAS. Yes sir! Yes, and you shall be.

CHARLES. How?

THOMAS. I don't know sir. I won't lie to you.

CHARLES. No, no I don't believe you would. You're too honest for your own good, Thomas. Which is exactly why I plucked you from the gutter! You're not like these other men, these Great Thinkers, you get things done!

(*The* **MEN** *glare at* **THOMAS**, *who shuffles uncomfortably.*)

THOMAS. Sir.

CHARLES. Oh let's run away together Thomas! You and I. Leave these dusty chaps to their endless scheming.

THOMAS. *(Amused.)* Where shall we go sir?

CHARLES. Reims! Get me to Reims! Where French Kings are crowned and the streets are paved with gold!

THOMAS. I wish I could sir. Your coronation there would be a beautiful thing to witness.

CHARLES. That it would... Paris? Get me to Paris at least? You know I do love Paris.

MAN TWO. We can't sir. The English have taken Paris!

CHARLES. What?!

MAN TWO. The English now occupy most of Northern France, sir. Meanwhile the Burgundians gain ground in the South.

MAN ONE. Bastard Burgundians! Traitors!

CHARLES. Oh when does it end? Nearly ninety years of war, and still no end in sight? Thomas?!

(Everyone stares at THOMAS.*)*

THOMAS. We need a miracle.

CHARLES. Is that it? We wait for a miracle? Marvellous.

(Silence. Stale quiet.)

Argh! Please! Someone suggest *something*, to relieve one's mind from this hellish dull nothingness before I burst into flames! I want adventure! I want entertainment! Oh entertain me Thomas!

THOMAS. Yes sir. What would you have me /

CHARLES. Oh no don't *ask* me! Don't ask what! Just *do*! Entertain me man!

*(*THOMAS *is shoved up to his feet. He stares, unsure what to do. He tries something, anything, he fails.* MAN THREE *bursts in, and* THOMAS *is relieved.)*

THOMAS. Oh thank god /

CHARLES. What is it?

MAN THREE. Sir! There is news, spreading fast among the common people, pleasing to the ear for it brings fresh courage to flagging spirits, new possibilities of hope so tantalising to the brokenhearted that it journeys quickly from tongue to tongue like wildfire!

CHARLES. Yes? What is it?

MAN THREE. There is a young woman, a simple maid, born in Domrémy. She travels here now, claiming to be chosen by God, to carry a message to you, yourself sir. She claims that God Almighty has called upon her, to lead an army, to save France!

MAN ONE. Goodness!

MAN TWO. Well the woman must be mad!

MAN ONE. Or a witch!

MAN THREE. So I thought myself! And yet the people flock to her, *hungry for hope*! She attracts more and more followers from each city she passes through. There is now a crowd following her every move and /

CHARLES. A crowd?

MAN ONE. A clump is probably more accurate sir, a, a cluster /

MAN TWO. A handful, no more, of simple folk, village people /

MAN ONE. Idiots! Foolish and fickle!

MAN TWO. They'd follow anyone anywhere!

CHARLES. Yes, well, the people do need *someone* to follow.

MAN ONE. Then how fortunate they are to have *you*, sir!

MAN TWO. Yes! The true King of France /

CHARLES. Not yet crowned. And the people do love a crown.

MAN THREE. There's more.

CHARLES. Go on.

MAN THREE. The crowds follow her, the the small, *small* group of *handful* of people /

CHARLES. Go on!

MAN THREE. They follow her sir, across war-torn country, and sing her praises. She journeys on horseback, for ten days now, or more.

CHARLES. Well, what of that? Why burst in here, all breathless, with urgent tales of girls on horseback? What is your purpose man?

MAN TWO. Yes! What of it? What of her?

MAN THREE. She's here.

CHARLES. Here?

MAN THREE. At the gate.

CHARLES. Now?!

MAN THREE. Now! Urgent to speak with you!

(This kicks up a ruckus among the MEN.)

CHARLES. Quickly! My robe! Put away these things! Quickly!

MAN ONE. Sir! You're not seriously considering meeting with her?!

CHARLES. Of course! This is the most exciting thing that's happened all year! My palms are sweating! Look! Actual moisture! For the first time in *months*! That's how under stimulating your company has been.

MAN ONE. Yes sir.

CHARLES. This strange visitor, a girl on horseback? Yes! It's positively thrilling!

MAN TWO. But sir! She could be a fraud!

MAN ONE. Or a mad woman! An assassin!

MAN TWO. Or a witch!

MAN ONE. Or the devil himself!

CHARLES. Or a monster from the deep dark depths of foolish man's imagination?! She's a *girl*! A simple *maid*! I want to meet with her.

MAN THREE. She was sent by Baudricourt.

MAN TWO. Baudricourt?!

MAN THREE. She has somehow convinced him. Stood outside his castle for *days* until he finally met with her. And then he became, so enraptured, by her testimony that he approved her journey here. Nay he supported it, he gave her his horse!

MAN TWO. Well the man must have been drunk!

MAN ONE. He does enjoy a drink.

CHARLES. Nevertheless I trust his judgement. And would be greatly surprised if he sent me a witch. *(To* **THOMAS.***)* Where is my robe?!

*(***THOMAS** *goes to find it.)*

MAN ONE. Sir, I must *insist* you reconsider /

MAN TWO. For your own safety /

MAN ONE. For the good of The People!

CHARLES. Oh! Must I always consider the good of The People? Can I not for a moment consider *myself*? *My* needs? *My* desires? I desire *adventure* and here it is! And yet you deny me it?!

MAN TWO. Deny you not, but protect you much sir /

CHARLES. From a *girl*?! Come now. I hardly need protection.

MAN ONE. We cannot be certain!

MAN TWO. It's too great a risk!

MAN ONE. Sir I must *insist*!

> (**CHARLES** *bats them away and pulls* **THOMAS**
> *aside.)*

CHARLES. Thomas?

THOMAS. There is a risk, sir, to your safety.

CHARLES. How annoying.

THOMAS. Such is the weight of responsibility, sir.

CHARLES. Ugh! I know! I just, oh, how I long sometimes, to be someone else, even just for a day!

THOMAS. Well, that's not a bad idea sir.

CHARLES. What's not?

THOMAS. Disguise yourself as another. Let another man play the part of Dauphin. And take the attack if there be one.

CHARLES. Brilliant!

> (**CHARLES** *turns to the* **OTHERS.**)

I am persuaded, that there can come no harm from granting an audience to this maid. However, to be secure, we're going to play a little game. We're going to pretend I am a simple man, a servant even. And someone else will play the part of me. Our young lady guest will be none the wiser and I shall be able to watch her in safety.

> (*The* **MEN** *applaud.)*

Now, who would like to be me?

(Every **MAN** *but* **THOMAS** *shoots up their hand.)*

Well. That's disconcerting.

*(***CHARLES*** *looks around and spots* **THOMAS**, *quietly minding his own business.)*

You.

THOMAS. No. Please, I desire it not I, I couldn't possibly /

CHARLES. Which is exactly why you must. You're the only one I truly trust, Thomas. There's not a drop of ambition in your skinny little body.

MAN THREE. She's coming! Quickly!

*(***CHARLES*** *takes off his robe and shoves it on the reluctant* **THOMAS**.*)*

THOMAS. Sir, please! I really would rather /

CHARLES. You'll be fine. You'll be fine! Just try and make me look handsome.

THOMAS. More handsome than your true self?

CHARLES. Oh, much more!

(The **MEN** *are scrambling to take their positions, directed by* **CHARLES** *as though posing for a photograph. Suddenly, the doors open, and everyone holds their breath. In walks* **JOAN**. *Silence. Everyone stares at* **JOAN***; the most bizarre thing they've ever seen. Someone gestures for* **JOAN** *to move towards* **THOMAS**. **JOAN** *walks towards him but stops, knowing it's not* **CHARLES**. **JOAN** *looks around at the* **MEN**, *devastated they'd lie, and turns to exit.)*

MAN ONE. Wait! Where are you going?!

MAN TWO. You wanted to see the Dauphin?!

JOAN. I do.

MAN TWO. Well, here he is!

JOAN. That's not him.

> *(Everyone is shocked. Some find it funny.* **JOAN** *is upset and angry.)*

MAN THREE. How do you know it's not him?!

JOAN. Please. I have an urgent message for the Dauphin.

MAN ONE. Then find him! He's here, somewhere.

JOAN. Sir, I beg you. This is not a game /

MAN TWO. Find him! And you can speak with him.

JOAN. Please, it's a matter of great importance!

MAN ONE. Then find him quickly.

> *(***JOAN*** looks at all the* **MEN,** *then closes their eyes.* **JOAN** *is still for a moment, and the* **MEN** *snicker.* **JOAN** *suddenly points at* **CHARLES,** *opens their eyes and looks at where they're pointing. Everyone is stunned.* **JOAN** *rushes over to* **CHARLES,** *kneels, and hugs his legs.)*

JOAN. Oh most noble Dauphin! God has sent me to help you and your kingdom!

> *(The* **MEN** *pull* **JOAN** *off him and hold them in the air.)*

CHARLES. *(Quietly.)* Are you mad?

JOAN. No sir, of sound mind, and sure footed.

CHARLES. And you are in earnest?

JOAN. I am, oh sir, I am! It is the Truth! I have been sent by God to deliver a message to you.

(This kicks up a ruckus among the **MEN.** **CHARLES** *quiets them all.* **JOAN** *is dropped to the floor but still held by the* **MEN.***)*

CHARLES. What is it?

JOAN. Sir, for your ears only. Please sir, some privacy?

MAN ONE. Absolutely not!

MAN TWO. Any message you intend to deliver may be heard by us all!

JOAN. Some of what I have to say may be heard by yourself /

MAN THREE. You'll do as you're told /

JOAN. But some words are only for the Dauphin /

MAN THREE. Or you'll be sent to the gallows /

JOAN. Soon to be crowned the true King of France!

CHARLES. How? How am I to be crowned?!

JOAN. I shall tell thee all sir, when we have privacy.

MAN TWO. No, I insist you share your message here.

JOAN. I am permitted to share some of it.

CHARLES. Go on.

JOAN. That part being, that I, Joan, am called upon by God to form a new army. To drive the English into the sea, and liberate France!

> *(This kicks up a big ruckus among the* **MEN.** **CHARLES** *signals for quiet, and they fall silent instantly.)*

CHARLES. Do you mock me?

JOAN. Oh, *no* sir! I adore thee, and humbly serve thee. And every word I speak is Truth! You *are* the True King of France. God told me so. I *am* going to crown you. And *together* we shall win the war. I have *one* year to do all this, so desire we begin immediately.

(Ruckus among the MEN. CHARLES *stares at* JOAN. THOMAS *stares at* JOAN. *The* MEN *talk to each other.)*

MAN ONE. Good God! Have you ever heard anything like it?!

MAN THREE. Never!

MAN ONE. I must say I don't approve of her tone. Speaking so boldly!

MAN THREE. Indeed. How old are you?

JOAN. Seventeen, or so... Oh be not distracted by my youth! I am in earnest, in all that I say and do, I *am* sent by God!

MAN THREE. She speaks well, for a farmer's daughter?

MAN ONE. Yes! And yet I doubt she can read, or write?

*(*JOAN *shakes their head.)*

Illiterate! A poor illiterate farm girl, leading the French army?

MAN THREE. Ridiculous!

MAN TWO. Yet she seems so confident?

MAN ONE. She's clearly mad! Or this is some clever design? An ambush!

MAN THREE. Yes! If we give her an army /

MAN ONE. *If* we give her? /

MAN THREE. She could lead it straight into the hands of the English!

MAN TWO. She's had no military training?

MAN THREE. Of course not! I doubt she's even held a sword. Could she even lift one?

MAN ONE. This is ridiculous! I can't believe we're even speaking with her /

THOMAS. And yet, she could be speaking Truth.

(*Everyone stares at* **THOMAS.**)

MAN THREE. What?!

MAN ONE. Nonsense!

MAN TWO. He's right.

MAN ONE. Goodness!

MAN TWO. Forget not the Virgin Mary! Also but a simple maid, used by our Good Lord to /

MAN ONE. I know the scripture! I am aware!

MAN TWO. Then can you truly say with absolute conviction that she is *not* a vessel of God?

(*The* **MEN** *fall silent.*)

CHARLES. What are you suggesting?

MAN TWO. Deliberation. Gentle, deliberation /

MAN ONE. Yes, yes we must take great care!

MAN TWO. We must tread carefully /

MAN ONE. Consider all the facts.

MAN THREE. Sleep on it, perhaps?

MAN TWO. Yes, take our time /

(**JOAN** *explodes with impatience. The* **MEN** *stare.*)

JOAN. Forgive me, I /.. We don't *have* much time! (*To* **THOMAS.**) The people are dying. Please!

THOMAS. I think we should listen to her.

MAN ONE. Oh yes?! And who are you to suggest anything? Remind me, which school it was you attended?

MAN TWO. Yes, what even *is* your position here at court? I'm unclear on your duties.

THOMAS. You disrespect me so regularly /

MAN TWO. And yet you persist in /

CHARLES. Gentlemen *please*! Quit squabbling. It's terribly dull.

ALL MEN. Sir.

CHARLES. Thomas, what do you suggest?

MAN ONE. Sir, might *I* suggest you consider consulting the men at court who are educated /

THOMAS. Rich you mean?

MAN TWO. Well yes, that too.

CHARLES. Gentlemen! Thomas?

THOMAS. Perhaps there is some use in listening to her. For we have clearly reached such terrible stalemate /

MAN ONE. Oh come on man! Our situation cannot be so desperate?! An army led by a *girl*?! A *peasant* girl?! It's laughable!

MAN TWO. It's humiliating! Sir, I won't have you humiliate yourself!

MAN THREE. No! Nor I!

MAN TWO. It's *madness*!

MAN ONE. It's impossible /

MAN THREE. Impossible!

MAN ONE. *Totally* impossible!

JOAN. A seed should not be able to push its way through the mud and *bloom*! And yet the flowers and trees prove it thus!

> *(Everyone stares at **JOAN**, who seems shocked their own mouth spoke.)*

CHARLES. Go on.

JOAN. I, forgive me, sir I /..

CHARLES. Go on.

JOAN. It's just that, well, the world is full of impossible truths! And, here I humbly offer you one more.

MAN TWO. But you're just /

JOAN. A girl! So you keep repeating! *(To **CHARLES**.)* But come sir, *you* have wisdom greater than this! For I know you are a man of God.

CHARLES. Barely.

JOAN. .

CHARLES. *(Shrugs.)* Faith is so easily lost at war.

JOAN. Then let me restore it for you! Rekindle the fire in your belly, for deep down you *know* I am speaking Truth!

MAN TWO. How *dare* you speak so boldly?

MAN ONE. Do not forget your place, little girl!

JOAN. *(Explodes.)* Oh please! Be not distracted by simple surface qualities when there are richer depths to explore! Look beyond this, *body*, look deeper! In truth I would that everyone would listen to their insides, for there the Kingdom of Heaven sings sweetly, and yet they do not *will* not it would seem so deafened by outside voices who play too loudly for them their ears full of nonsense cloud their eyes until they cannot see what is so plainly offered /

CHARLES. Which is?

JOAN. That I, the unlikely messenger, carry an impossible Truth, for you!

CHARLES. What is your message?

JOAN. My Lord, for your ears only.

> (**CHARLES** *is stunned, and yet he nods. The* **MEN** *are horrified.*)

CHARLES. My private chambers are through here /

MAN THREE. Sir?!

MAN ONE. Sir I really must *insist*!

MAN TWO. What if she's a *fraud*?!

CHARLES. What if she's not?

> (**CHARLES** *exits with* **JOAN.** *The* **MEN** *pace.*
> *Eventually,* **JOAN** *and* **CHARLES** *re-enter.*
> *There's something different about* **CHARLES'**
> *face, like he's seen something extraordinary.*)

Thomas, prepare lodgings and food for this young woman. We are to keep her safe. She is to live with us here in the tower whilst we make arrangements.

MAN TWO. Arrangements?

CHARLES. To make an attack on the English.

> (*The* **MEN** *kick off, overlapping each other.*)

MAN TWO. Good heavens /

MAN ONE. This is preposterous /

MAN THREE. Unbelievable /

MAN ONE. What *happened* in there /

MAN TWO. What did she say to you /

CHARLES. As sudden as all this seems, I assure you of my sincerity.

MAN TWO. But sir! We *must* know what has been discussed between you!

CHARLES. I may not speak of it.

MAN ONE. Sir, I must insist /

MAN THREE. For your own safety!

CHARLES. I may not speak of it. Don't ask me again.

MAN ONE. Sir, sir please! Please! I *must* protest! I will not have you *humiliate* yourself!

MAN THREE. No! Nor I!

MAN ONE. Your good name tarnished by, by whatever this is, wilful ambition or youthful arrogance or /

MAN TWO. How do we know she's even capable?!

JOAN. Orléans.

(*The* **MEN** *stare at* **JOAN.**)

CHARLES. What?

JOAN. Orléans.

THOMAS. It's a city, along the Loire River, not far from /

CHARLES. I know what it is! What of it?!

JOAN. Let me show you. At Orléans.

THOMAS. What is the situation there?

JOAN. Desperate. The English have surrounded the city walls, starving the people inside until they surrender.

MAN TWO. How do you know?

JOAN. I passed through there, barely two days ago. I saw them! I was there!

MAN TWO. Well, I /

JOAN. The citizens have been holding on, heroically, with little to no provisions, for *months*! Baudricourt told me they have repeatedly begged for aid. They are desperate for supplies /

MAN ONE. The treasury is empty! We cannot send more!

JOAN. They cannot hold for much longer! The entire city is starving, women and children too, praying for your help. And the English sit around the city walls, just *waiting* for them to surrender.

THOMAS. And if they do?

MAN THREE. It doesn't bear thinking about!

JOAN. If the English take Orléans they'll have opened the gates to southern France. They'll flood through the country like a plague. We'd lose the war instantly.

> *(The* MEN *shuffle, unsure.* JOAN *stares at them, impatient.)*

I can help them, I can do it! I'll break into the city, bring them supplies, raise the siege, drive out the English!

CHARLES. How?!

JOAN. By God's grace.

> *(The* MEN *stare at* JOAN.*)*

CHARLES. If she were to succeed?

MAN ONE. Impossible!

MAN THREE. Then the English defences would be severely damaged /

CHARLES. Yes /

MAN THREE. Gaining us vital ground!

MAN TWO. It'd be our first victory in months!

THOMAS. And if she should fail?

MAN ONE. *When* she fails! Humiliating us all as she /

THOMAS. If she should fail?

JOAN. Death.

(*Silence.*)

CHARLES. So be it. Orléans, as a test, a month from today.

JOAN. A month?! But sir, I am ready now!

CHARLES. A month to prepare is barely enough time as it is.

JOAN. But sir, please /

CHARLES. Believe me, you'll need it. We'll have someone make you some armour, and get you a sword.

THOMAS. I'll arrange it sir.

CHARLES. Thank you Thomas.

MAN ONE. Sir! Sir! I cannot support this!

MAN THREE. No sir nor I! We cannot *test* her in the field like this! Men's lives are at risk!

MAN TWO. Yes let us be assured first, that she is not a witch! I must *insist* the maid is examined!

MAN ONE. Yes! Let the ecclesiastics meet with her!

MAN TWO. And the judges! And the theologians!

MAN ONE. Yes, they can decide if she is to be trusted.

MAN THREE. And if she is indeed even *capable* of leading an army to battle!

THOMAS. You are willing to be examined?

JOAN. If I must.

CHARLES. Well then. Let's begin. Tomorrow at dawn.

JOAN. I'm ready now!

CHARLES. Tomorrow. Get some rest.

*(The **MEN** exit. Once **JOAN** is sure they're*
alone, they turn to us and explode into
shocked giggles. They try to calm and focus.
They speak to God through us. They begin
praying formally, but the fizz soon bursts
through.)

JOAN. Oh God, I humbly, offer myself, to thee, I /.. I /.. I
was *so brave*?! Oh my God did you see me?! Did you
see?! I was *so brave*?! My body, stood, so *still*?! And so
strong?! And so, *sure*?! Not even the slightest tremor in
my hand, no restlessness or unease in my skin no, no
breathlessness or, or panicked /.. but standing, *proud*?
Like, like I *owned* the very ground I stood upon? Like I
deserved to be there, unquestionably, just, *there.* Being
heard. They listened! Is this what it's like to be a man?
And oh! I spoke so well! Those words that poured
through me? Beautiful words! And the way my mouth
formed the sounds?! I /.. Oh! What honour, what an
honour it is, to be your, channel. So, so humbled am I
to have experienced that, magic! Cus that, that was not
me. Obviously, I /.. Impossible, completely impossible!
And yet, today, just for one moment, I was the place
through which the Infinite expressed itself. And
express itself, *you did*! Oh, those words?! You poured
through me with such clarity and oh, such confidence!
Such convincing confidence I, *I* am convincing, *they*
are convinced?! Did you see their faces?! ...But, oh,
oh no. Oh no this must end here, I can't repeat that I
/.. I need to go home I, I need to /.. Oh God, please
help me, I, surely this is some terrible mistake? Like,
of all the vessels to choose from, am I really the best
choice?! Not of course that I'm questioning you, I just
/.. War? /.. Me? /.. I, Joan, I am to lead, the French
Army, into battle? I, little Joan? *Are you mad?!* ...And
yet... I hardly dare say it, but, it's undeniable. This tiny
flicker of a flame, deep in my belly that desires this, that
believes... Why not I? It is a thing that must be done.
And someone must be the one to do it. And the doing

of it is more vital than the man who does it, or woman or /.. So why not I? Why not Joan? Joan the warrior?

(**JOAN** *giggles.*)

Nah! Nah, come now Joan, be serious, be serious!

(*They try this on for size. They like it.*)

Yeah! Stern! And, macho! Yeah! Yeah that's, yeah much better I /

THOMAS. Madam?

JOAN. Oh!

THOMAS. Forgive me! I did not mean to interrupt you praying. I can return /

JOAN. It's fine! I was almost finished.

(**THOMAS** *hovers, awkwardly.*)

You supported me? With those men, you /

THOMAS. I've never seen anything like you!

JOAN. .

THOMAS. Like *that*, I mean, *that*, what you just did, with those men that was, Quite Something! I mean / (*He checks no one is listening.*) You stormed in like a Thunderbolt! You must be /.. I mean, that was, A Lot!

JOAN. Yes.

THOMAS. Yes! Can I ask, are you all right? After all that, are you /

JOAN. Yes, thank you.

(*They smile at each other. A connection. Then* **THOMAS** *remembers himself.*)

THOMAS. Right, yes well. Will you require supper?

JOAN. Yes. Yes please, thank you.

THOMAS. Will you attend the dining hall or have it here?

JOAN. Here, please, thank you.

THOMAS. I'll bring it.

JOAN. Thank you.

THOMAS. .

JOAN. What?

THOMAS. You don't need to thank me.

JOAN. I do and I shall. Always.

THOMAS. Okay.

> (**THOMAS** *stares at* **JOAN.** *A little queer nod, a smile. He exits.* **JOAN** *turns to us.*)

JOAN. Oh God, what a laugh you must be havin'! For what madness is stirred up in these men?! I mean if *I* wasn't the one doin' the stirrin' I would maybe have a little more space to enjoy it, it's true. But here I am, the cause of their disruption, and hardly believing it myself. Oh, what a day! My head is spinnin'!

> (**JOAN** *stares at us, wide-eyed with wonder. They giggle. They get scared. They giggle again. They pull themself together.*)

Focus Joan, focus.

> (**JOAN** *meditates, quietly alone.*)

Scene Two

(Around **JOAN***, the stage is filled with* **MEN***. Drummers enter, and* **JOAN** *bounces to their beat.* **JOAN** *explores what their body can do. The* **MEN** *stare as* **JOAN** *grows in confidence.* **JOAN** *stops, suddenly shy.* **MAN THREE** *attempts to teach* **JOAN** *the basics of sword fighting, but* **JOAN***'s uninterested in his instruction.* **JOAN** *closes their eyes and is still for a moment, then is suddenly a brilliant swordsman. The* **MEN** *stare in astonishment, then turn to each other to discuss* **JOAN***.* **JOAN** *rolls their eyes and turns to us, they speak to God through us.)*

JOAN. *(To us.)* The men are talkin' about me like I'm not here. They do this a lot.

MAN TWO. Well, she's speaking sound sentences.

MAN THREE. Yes, yes I do not consider her mad.

MAN TWO. Nor I. The question is /

MAN ONE. Which man does possess her?

MAN TWO. Yes.

MAN THREE. Yes, is it the Devil? Or our Good Lord?

JOAN. *(To us.)* Oh God, give me patience!

MAN TWO. She is wild, around the eyes, I've noticed.

MAN ONE. Yes, I've noticed that too.

MAN THREE. She is, presumably, a virgin?

MAN TWO. One would assume so.

MAN THREE. We'll have it verified. And her teeth?

MAN ONE. All present I believe.

JOAN. *(To us.)* They go on and on about me and I'm standing right in front of them, politely waitin' for at least *one* of them to remember that I am in fact a human! Standing right here! And I do in fact have a *mind* and a *mouth* and perhaps they could direct their questions *at me*, rather than speakin' *about* me, *around* me, over the top of my head?!

MAN ONE. She's fairly tall. And appears strong for her sex.

MAN THREE. Yes. She is *perhaps* physically able.

MAN TWO. Ah yes, but does she have the mind for it?

MAN THREE. Undoubtedly not. Which makes it all the more bewildering.

MAN ONE. Yes, how *is* she able to speak so well?!

JOAN. *(To us.)* The audacity of it?! The arrogance?! Arguing my validity, questionin' my divinity, ignoring my humanity and assumin' I've got nothin' to say?! Why, cus I'm poor? Cus I'm in this body? Cus I ain't never been taught to read or write? Not got a penny to my name. Look, I'll be the first to say I'm nobody from nowhere, not goin' nowhere, not got nothin' so got nothin' to lose. Except my life. For let's not forget, I could be killed for standing right here. And yet here I am, being brave, because *you* told me to. And if that's not enough to convince man then, I dunno what they're expecting me to do? Walk on water?

> (**JOAN** *looks at the* **MEN**, *who are in a huddle, bustling like chickens, arguing in loud whispers.*)

Look at them! These are the men that run your country? ...Okay. Watch this yeah, I'll try again.

> (**JOAN** *turns to the* **MEN**.)

Erm, excuse me sirs? Excuse me?

(JOAN is ignored, so turns back to us. They shrug and roll their eyes. They absentmindedly start moving with the sword, they're good.)

I must admit, I'm enjoying this. Feels, so good! My body making all these shapes it's never been allowed to make. And I'm faster than I thought I'd be, able to shift across space like, like I've done this before? Like my body *knows*, before I do? Like somehow it's already there, under my skin, all this potential and passion and, power? I've got, power? Here, in my fingertips I /.. I can feel it, here, in my chest I /.. I've got power! Why didn't anyone ever tell me?!

(JOAN dances a little, the power fizzing up through their body. The MEN stare. JOAN feels their gaze and stops, suddenly apologetic. The MEN frown, and go back to their huddle, muttering.)

CHARLES. Quiet!

(CHARLES appears and locks eyes with JOAN across the space. The air is fizzy.)

Give her a chance.

JOAN. *(To us.)* And everyone stares. And, I start again with the sword and I /.. I can see it all so clearly! I can see Orléans, I can see us winning, I can see it all! And the Dauphin watches me seeing it and somehow he must see it too, because he agrees! Oh my God, he's *just like me*! He sees me, I am seen.

(CHARLES and JOAN smile at each other. The MEN see it and are horrified.)

CHARLES. Very good!

MAN TWO. Sir?!

MAN THREE. Sir no, no we're not finished /

MAN ONE. This is *outrageous*!

YOLANDE. Come gentlemen, are you *still* so intimidated by awesome women?

> (**YOLANDE** *appears from nowhere and sweeps across the stage, closely followed by a heavily pregnant* **MARIE**. *They are fearsome, and gorgeous. The* **MEN** *bow low, instantly undone.* **CHARLES** *chuckles, amused.* **JOAN**'s *jaw hits the floor.*)

For is it not one of the great Truths, that in this world of men, if you want something done well, you hire a woman.

CHARLES. Women serve men very well, it's true.

MARIE. Serve them? Cover for them you mean! Where were you today at court?

CHARLES. I, I was /

MARIE. Once again I preside over the council of state?

CHARLES. Yes, well /

MARIE. In my condition? *Hours* spent in *dusty* courtrooms juggling ugly men's egos, finding solutions for *your* problems, granting myself power of attorney and signing acts on *your* behalf?

CHARLES. Well yes, which is why I made you Lieutenant Marie! Lieutenant and my Queen! My beautiful queen!

MARIE. Don't touch me. I'm hot, my feet ache, get me water.

CHARLES. Water! Someone fetch her water!

YOLANDE. She asked you.

> (*Everyone stares.* **CHARLES** *exits.*)

Now, where is she? Where's this wonder woman? Ah, Joan! It is my great pleasure to meet you. We were most intrigued by this young lady who has caused such a stir among these men, and I knew instantly that we'd be friends.

JOAN. *(Bowing and blushing.)* Ma'am.

YOLANDE. I am Yolande of Aragon. I run both the house of Anjou and the house of Valois, and I finance all operations here. That means I hold the purse strings, I guide my wayward son-in-law Charles, and I advise these men who sit safely in the palm of my hand.

MARIE. It's said my mother has a man's heart in a woman's body.

YOLANDE. *(Smiling.)* Perhaps.

MARIE. *(To* **JOAN.***)* Something I think you can relate to?

JOAN. *(Bowing and blushing.)* Ma'am.

YOLANDE. My daughter, Marie.

CHARLES. My wife! My beautiful wife!

> *(***CHARLES** *appears with water, expecting a thank you. ***MARIE** *doesn't look at him, takes it, downs it and gives him the glass.)*

And this, in here, is my son /

YOLANDE. It's a girl.

MARIE. Mother.

CHARLES. How do you /

YOLANDE. Oh it's obvious!

MARIE. Mother, please. *(To* **CHARLES.***)* It's a girl.

CHARLES. Oh.

MARIE. Oh?

CHARLES. Oh, marvellous! That's, that's *marvellous* that's /

MARIE. Sit down.

CHARLES. Yes.

>   (**CHARLES** *sulks in the corner.*)

MARIE. Joan, it's my pleasure to meet you. Do you have
>   everything you need? Are these men being terribly
>   dull?

MAN ONE. We are in the process of questioning her, ma'am.

YOLANDE. And doing so extremely effectively, no doubt.

MAN ONE. I /..

YOLANDE. Well? Don't let us stop you.

MAN ONE. /..

YOLANDE. Proceed.

>   (**MAN ONE** *is suddenly flustered. He looks to
>   the other* **MEN** *for help, and they avoid his
>   gaze.*)

MAN ONE. Yes I. /.. Erm. Joan. Is it, true, erm /

YOLANDE. How is it that God communicates with you
>   so directly, Joan? We long to know this *experience* of
>   hearing God. Can you speak more of this?

>   (*The* **MEN** *stare.* **JOAN** *feels the tension.*)

JOAN. I, I don't know the words, ma'am.

YOLANDE. You do. Of course you do.

JOAN. /..

MARIE. Joan, we believe you. Just, tell us how it feels.

MAN ONE. Feels?!

(**YOLANDE** *glares, and* **MAN ONE** *shrinks.* **YOLANDE** *nods at* **JOAN**. **MARIE** *smiles encouragingly.* **JOAN** *closes their eyes.*)

JOAN. Calm. God feels calm, and clear, and suddenly oh so very simple. Despite everything just, sudden Truth, suddenly *there*! And with it, absolute conviction, I just *know*, I suddenly just *know*? /..

(**JOAN** *opens their eyes to check they're listening. Everyone is hanging onto every word.*)

And, and incredible energy! Pouring through me, infinite light and colours and wind and I can do anything! The calm is, fueling me? Giving me power and it's *new* but also the *oldest*, wisest most true *deepest* part of me, deep in my belly in my bones right in the root of the root of me.

(**YOLANDE** *nods.* **MARIE** *smiles. These three share some connection.*)

CHARLES. Well, is that it? Are we all satisfied?

YOLANDE. *(Patronising.)* Not quite Charles.

MAN ONE. No sir madam I, I have more questions!

YOLANDE. So do I /

CHARLES. So do I!

(**YOLANDE** *raises her eyebrows.* **CHARLES** *falters.*)

I /.. Thomas?

(*The* **MEN** *roll their eyes and whisper to each other.* **MARIE** *is embarrassed.*)

THOMAS. Sir?

CHARLES. In your opinion, how is she doing?

>*(THOMAS is embarrassed to be asked. The other*
>*MEN scowl at him. MARIE can't bear it.)*

MARIE. Why are you asking *him*?!

>*(YOLANDE raises a hand, and MARIE falls*
>*silent. THOMAS feels the tension.)*

THOMAS. I, am not in charge of this operation sir, I /

CHARLES. Yes you are. Answer my question.

THOMAS. Excellently, sir, on all accounts. Nimble-footed
and fast with a sword. As though she has done nothing
else all her life.

CHARLES. And the military techniques?

THOMAS. Her mind is sharp despite her lack of education.

YOLANDE. Oh of course it is!

THOMAS. She's a keen student, quick to learn, humble.

YOLANDE. That too was obvious just by looking at her!

THOMAS. Ma'am.

CHARLES. What about these dusty court chaps? How's she
been fairing up against them and their questions?

THOMAS. She's creating marvel and wonder in all! In
even the most sceptical man. Every single one of them
moved to tears. Such is the spiritual beauty she does
possess.

YOLANDE. Yes. There is something here, something /..

MARIE. *(Pushing THOMAS aside.)* New.

YOLANDE. Yes.

>*(YOLANDE and MARIE stare at JOAN, who*
>*tries to breathe.)*

MAN TWO. New or not, she has still failed to prove that she is capable of leading thousands of men into battle!

YOLANDE. Oh she's capable. I believe it.

(**JOAN** *smiles. The* **MEN** *are horrified.*)

Yes, I think she's just what we need. The people will love her, and follow her.

MARIE. Undoubtedly.

YOLANDE. A new weapon!

MARIE. Unexpected.

YOLANDE. Surprising! Who will fight for us?

JOAN. To the death!

YOLANDE. Haha yes! A little firecracker!

CHARLES. I told you! I told you!

MARIE. *(Dismissive.)* Yes darling.

MAN ONE. *(Exploding.)* Madam! Please! We have our concerns!

YOLANDE. Of course you do.

MAN TWO. Please, madam, let us show you the alternative plans we have drawn up?

YOLANDE. Very well.

(**YOLANDE** *and* **MARIE** *follow the* **MEN** *to the side of the stage.* **JOAN** *panics.*)

JOAN. Where are they going? What's happening?!

THOMAS. They're just consulting some plans. Everything is well, Joan, they're pleased with your progress.

JOAN. So we can get on with it now?

THOMAS. Soon. They just need to /

JOAN. No, now! I am instructed *by God* to lead the charge!

THOMAS. This I know, Joan, for you have cried it so, repeatedly /

JOAN. Well cry it some more shall I, until I am heard! *Why* do these men delay at every opportunity? It is as though they *enjoy* delaying more than anything else? Their favourite pastime, a devotion of delaying?!

THOMAS. Yes, I know it can feel like that, I *(Checks no one is listening.)* I too, sometimes, am frustrated by their speed, or lack thereof.

JOAN. *(Fizzing up and over.)* And yet you do *nothing* to change them? You're *passive*?! And *polite*! Which makes *you*, just like *them*, you're just the same!

THOMAS. I'm not I'm not like them I'm *like you*!

> *(They see one another. THOMAS collects himself and checks no one is listening. JOAN struggles to regulate.)*

I, I am not married, I /.. I don't come from money. I was chosen by Charles to join this court, and yet still I am not respected by these men. I do not always feels heard /

JOAN. *(Impatient.)* Then speak louder! They need your insight! You are closer to the people they are serving.

THOMAS. Louder isn't always an option. You don't understand, I wouldn't just lose my job, I'd lose my head! We have to tread carefully, play them at their own game, one step at a time. I can show you how to do that if you /

JOAN. That sounds long.

THOMAS. It can be /

JOAN. I don't have time for that. Why won't they let me go to war?! Have I not shown that I am capable?! Every task they set me I complete! And always obediently, and never complain! What more do they want?!

THOMAS. Time. They need time to /

JOAN. They've had time! Plenty of it, too much! Time to rip through land and burn our homes and scorch the earth?! I'm offering freedom, a new freedom! How much more time do they need?!

THOMAS. Time to catch up with you! What you propose is radical! These men are dusty in their traditions, it's true, and therefore need time to reorganise their thoughts. To see the world as you see /

JOAN. Why is that so difficult?! Their intellect far exceeds mine and yet they struggle to see basic Truth?

THOMAS. They cannot believe it without some proof!

JOAN. Give me an army and I shall prove it thus!

THOMAS. They won't give you an army until they are confident in their vision of you leading one.

JOAN. Is that it? They can't imagine me doing it?

THOMAS. Of course! No offence but, you're a *girl*, and /

JOAN. Right.

> (**JOAN** *starts hacking at their hair with their sword.*)

THOMAS. Joan! Stop! Stop stop stop Stop STOP!

> (**YOLANDE** *and* **MARIE** *rush over, followed by all the* **MEN**.)

JOAN. You're right, they'll never listen to me!

YOLANDE. Goodness!

JOAN. Men's eyes block their ears!

THOMAS. Don't! You'll be *killed*! Stop!

MAN ONE. As I suspected! She's mad!

MAN TWO. She's a witch!

MAN THREE. Get her out!

YOLANDE. Quiet!

MAN TWO. But madam it is a *sin*!

JOAN. Says who?

MAN TWO. God!

JOAN. Not my God!

MAN ONE. Heresy! That's *heresy*!

YOLANDE. Oh hush!

MAN THREE. But madam, the *law*! It is *forbidden* for women to /

JOAN. This is my law! This gut instinct? It's so loud, it's undeniable!

YOLANDE. Fascinating!

JOAN. I must alter what they *see*, so they can *hear* me!

(**MARIE** *approaches* **JOAN.**)

MARIE. Joan?

CHARLES. Marie, careful!

JOAN. Short like a soldier's!

MARIE. Joan /

JOAN. I must be *heard*! They *must* hear me!

MARIE. Yes! Yes okay Joan, okay! But, perhaps a smaller blade? And a mirror, would be useful?

(**JOAN** *agrees. The world spins.* **JOAN** *cuts their hair, and with the help of* **MARIE** *and* **THOMAS**, *they put on an army uniform. It's a very practical decision, with no emotional* *investment. Until they spot themself in the mirror.* JOAN *stares.* JOAN *smiles.* JOAN *poses, and plays. They're experimenting, enjoying, expanding.* MARIE *and* THOMAS *watch in awe.* CHARLES *and* YOLANDE *enter, closely followed by the* MEN. *They stop dead at the sight of* JOAN. *Everyone holds their breath.)*

MAN TWO. *This* sir! Surely *this* is all the proof you need?!

MAN THREE. Yes, this confirms it!

CHARLES. Yes it does.

MAN ONE. She's a mad woman!

CHARLES. No. She's a warrior.

(YOLANDE *steps forward, holding white and gold armour for* JOAN.)

YOLANDE. An army is assembled. Eighteen thousand men. Can you lead them?

JOAN. In the name of God, I can.

CHARLES. Then onwards! To Orléans!

Scene Three

> *(Drummers begin a military beat.* **THOMAS**
> *helps* **JOAN** *put on the armour, and stands*
> *back to admire them.* **JOAN** *looks the nuts,*
> *and feels like a rockstar. The world spins, and*
> **SOLDIERS** *enter the stage.* **JOAN** *moves their*
> *body to suggest something, but the* **MEN** *ignore*
> **JOAN** *and move their own way.* **JOAN** *tries*
> *again, but again is ignored. The drumming*
> *suddenly stops.)*

JOAN. We must push *forward!*

> *(The* **MEN** *ignore* **JOAN***.)*

Forward, I say! We must break into the city of Orléans!
...Why do you disobey me? I am here to lead you!
Attack the city walls!

SOLDIER ONE. Listen love. See that there? That's an
English garrison. One of many, that surround the
whole city. Hundreds of troops are stationed at each
one. We ain't gettin' through that.

JOAN. We will! We must!

SOLDIER ONE. And up there? See those archers, all along
the city wall?

SOLDIER TWO. There's no way we're gettin' even close /

SOLDIER ONE. No /

SOLDIER TWO. Let alone through 'em!

JOAN. We have to! We *need* to break inside the city of
Orléans!

SOLDIER ONE. Impossible!

JOAN. Bring them supplies /

SOLDIER TWO. No chance /

JOAN. Feed the people! Raise arms *with* them! Then together burst back outwards attacking the English who surround the city!

SOLDIER ONE. We've been trying to do, exactly that, for *months*. And I'm tellin' yer, it's fuckin' impossible!

JOAN. Nothing is impossible! *(To all the* **MEN**.*)* Come! Come! We must attack!

SOLDIER THREE. We cannot!

JOAN. We must! I was here just barely a few days ago and I *promised* them I would return! They are *waiting* for me! I can help them!

SOLDIER THREE. How can you, when we could not? What makes you think you will succeed where we men have failed?

JOAN. I am fuelled by God!

SOLDIER THREE. God left this country long ago. Left us men in the mud.

JOAN. Never, never! To arms! To arms I say! Quickly! Why do you delay? The people are *starving*!

SOLDIER ONE. *(Explodes.)* We fuckin' know that! Do you not think we fuckin' know that?!

SOLDIER TWO. *(Trying to calm him.)* Hey hey easy!

SOLDIER ONE. We've been trying to help them! For *months* now! We've sat here, in the mud, hearing them screaming, and there's *fuck all* we can do about it?! We've asked for help, over and over, and what does he send us? *(Suddenly right in* **JOAN**'s *face.)* A girl?!

JOAN. *(Trying to stay calm.)* I have eighteen thousand men under my command.

SOLDIER ONE. *(Cold.)* Well you got one less now.

(The **MEN** *turn their backs on* **JOAN**.*)*

JOAN. Forward. *Forward*, I say!

THOMAS. Joan, perhaps we /

JOAN. Why do you disobey me? I am here to lead you!

SOLDIER THREE. No offence love, but I won't be led by a girl.

JOAN. I am sent by the Dauphin!

SOLDIER TWO. To be fair I've always questioned his judgement.

JOAN. And commit treason by doing so!

DUNOIS. So be it. But first, a battle here must be won.

> (**DUNOIS** *sweeps onto the stage, macho and magnificent.*)

SOLDIER ONE. Dunois!

SOLDIER THREE. Thank God! You have returned!

SOLDIER TWO. We are in desperate need sir, of some strong leadership!

SOLDIER THREE. From a *Man*, with experience!

SOLDIER ONE. For we are, inexplicably, led into battle by a *girl*, of all things!

DUNOIS. So I heard. And hardly dare believe it. But, alas! It seems the Dauphin has truly lost his mind.

JOAN. .

DUNOIS. *(To* **THOMAS.**) You are?

THOMAS. Thomas. The Dauphin's adviser.

DUNOIS. Oh aye, did you advise this?

THOMAS. No! No I actually /

DUNOIS. I don't need to know, son. *(To* **SOLDIER ONE.**) What is our situation?

SOLDIER ONE. Disastrous!

SOLDIER THREE. Outnumbered and exhausted.

DUNOIS. Right.

SOLDIER TWO. The Dauphin has *finally* sent us supplies!

DUNOIS. Have *you* men refuelled?

SOLDIER ONE. Barely.

DUNOIS. Give our men food and drink first.

SOLDIER ONE. Sir.

    *(***SOLDIER ONE*** runs off.)*

DUNOIS. Then we'll see about feeding those poor souls.

SOLDIER THREE. We have boats, full of supplies for them, here and here.

SOLDIER TWO. But they can't move! Blocked by the English archers, who have the advantage of the hillside.

SOLDIER THREE. Excellent marksmen they are too.

DUNOIS. And the drawbridge?

SOLDIER THREE. Burned.

DUNOIS. Of course. And I don't suppose we could attempt the east wing, here?

    *(***SOLDIER ONE*** runs back on.)*

SOLDIER TWO. We can't, we can't move our position at all.

SOLDIER THREE. We are surrounded by foot soldiers. Here, here and here.

DUNOIS. Right. So, lemme get this straight. We have less soldiers /

SOLDIER TWO. Less swords /

SOLDIER ONE. Less arrows /

SOLDIER THREE. And Joan.

DUNOIS. Great! Well, this is as good a place as any to die, I suppose.

JOAN. We must push forward! Now! We must attack the city walls immediately!

DUNOIS. Go home little one. This really is no place for a maid.

JOAN. I am sent by God! I AM SENT BY GOD! Why won't you listen?!

DUNOIS. I have no idea, for volume is clearly no issue.

(The **MEN** *laugh.* **JOAN** *is furious.)*

JOAN. You think this is funny? Our people are starving to death, in there, right now! And you men stand around doing nothing?

DUNOIS. Oh aye, we sit and do nothin' too. Lie down sometimes.

JOAN. What?!

THOMAS. *(Pulling* **JOAN** *aside.)* Joan, you've got to learn to work with him. I know he's a little rough 'round the edges, but he's very experienced /

JOAN. Then he should be *doing something*!

DUNOIS. Wouldn't you prefer a bit of baking? Needlecraft?

(He winks. **JOAN** *glares at him. He consults the maps.)*

Now, if my memory serves me...yes, there! There is a brook, here, gentlemen. I suggest, tomorrow, we could manoeuvre our men /

JOAN. Tomorrow?! No, we must push on immediately! I *urge* us to attack! *Here!* On the Bastille of St. Laurent, to the west! We shall take our men, here, up through the hills and /

SOLDIER THREE. That Bastille is the strongest of all!

SOLDIER TWO. Yes! And our men need rest!

JOAN. What?! There is no time for *rest*! We must attack!

DUNOIS. We *must* rest! The men are exhausted.

JOAN. We must *attack* whilst the *English* are exhausted!

DUNOIS. When we're exhausted good men die. I'm not having that.

JOAN. No you'll just let civilians die instead?

SOLDIER ONE. Ooh, stop now! Before I do something I regret /

JOAN. Unlikely! For you love to avoid taking any action! You indulge in *every* opportunity to delay! Call yourselves men of war?

DUNOIS. *(Suddenly serious.)* We do. And as commander here *I* shall decide the course of action.

MEN. Sir.

DUNOIS. Tonight, we rest /

JOAN. No /

DUNOIS. Tomorrow, we'll advance. Carefully at dawn, whilst the English lie sleeping.

SOLDIER THREE. Like we did at Voyennes?

DUNOIS. Exactly.

> (**SOLDIER THREE** *smiles at the memory and nods in agreement.* **JOAN** *paces, frustrated.*)

If we can manoeuvre our men, quietly, across this brook, then we're in with a chance of clearing the English on the south bank before they're even awake enough to know what's happening.

SOLDIER TWO. A surprise attack!

SOLDIER THREE. Yes! And the English are weakest there.

SOLDIER ONE. I agree. Brilliant!

DUNOIS. Very well. At sunrise, we shall begin.

JOAN. No, *now*!

DUNOIS. Tomorrow.

JOAN. We should attack *now*!

ALL MEN. TOMORROW!

> (*The* **MEN** *start to make up places to sleep.*
> **JOAN** *spins, angry and desperate.*)

JOAN. Get up! Get up! We must attack! Now! Get up! Get up!

DUNOIS. Rest, little one. Tomorrow is a big day.

> (**JOAN** *turns to us.*)

JOAN. ARGH! These MEN?! Oh GOD, I *HATE THEM*! I hate *this*! I hate I hate I hate I hate I *hate* this *body* I am in! For clearly it is the cause of their disdain! Their disrespect, their deafness to my words, a *complete refusal* to hear me even as I speak *the word of God*?! What are they so afraid of?! They barely even look at me?! To be fair I can barely look at myself, I /.. Sometimes I feel, so free! Like I completely forget the skin I'm in and I'm floating outside of myself and then *crash*! I'm reminded, people think I'm a girl. They look at me, and yeah okay, if you looked at me and saw my body you'd see the body of a girl so you'd probably assume I'm a girl too, but I'm not! I promise you I'm not I, I, I don't know what I am, I /..

Ugh! These men?! So *astounded* by the idea of a *girl* doing a man's work, of a *girl* at war, and I want to tell them *no*! No I, I'm not a, oh! Oh god! Did you, did you think I'm a? Hahaha! You thought I was a *girl*? How funny! How *hilarious*! How terribly heartbreaking.

And let me be clear, I love girls. I *love* girls. I think I am actually a bit in love with a girl that I sit behind in church, I mean she smiled at me once and the world span faster and her name is Jessica and her hair smells like summer but that's a whole other /.. Like some other time I /.. What I mean to say is, please don't mistake me! I have no intention of adding to the weight of shame being put on girls, girls are great! Girls are brilliant! Girls are fuckin' fantastic! There's nothin' wrong with being a girl! Except if you're not. Except if everyone insists on calling you one, when you're not, then there's *everything* wrong, then everything *is* wrong everything is war! /.. Yeah! Oh my god yeah, everything is war, every day, and like, I mean, these men? They honestly think I'm a stranger to war? Are they that blind? Cus like, like isn't it true, that to be born in a female body, in *this* world of men is to be at war every day?! And *then*, to be born a girl when you're *not* a girl? That's civil war. Bloody and brutal.

Oh god, why did you put me in *this* body? /.. I have so much work to do, and so little time! I'm not waiting for these men. Nah! Nah, if I have to do this on my own then I will.

> (**JOAN** *stands, determined to leave and fight alone.* **THOMAS** *appears from nowhere and stops them.*)

THOMAS. Wait! Wait wait wait!

JOAN. I cannot wait! I cannot wait a moment longer! I am called to fight!

THOMAS. Joan no! Stop, stop!

> (**THOMAS** *grabs* **JOAN** *and holds them back.* **JOAN** *growls, frustrated.*)

You cannot fight alone! You'll be killed, instantly! It'd be a pointless suicide! And then these men would win!

(**JOAN** *stops.*)

THOMAS. Just wait, wait! Wait *one* night! *One night!* Give people time to grow, time to catch up with you!

JOAN. Why does it take so long?!

THOMAS. We don't have what you have! We don't have your insight, we can't see it. We need you to show us! Please!

> (**JOAN** *sulks and slumps down on the edge of the stage.* **THOMAS** *sits gingerly next to* **JOAN.** *He waits in silence for them to soften.*)

Have you ever seen the stars shine so brightly?

JOAN. .

THOMAS. I mean, whoever painted that is showing off!

> (**THOMAS** *laughs,* **JOAN** *doesn't.*)

It's so vast! Makes me feel small.

> (**JOAN** *sighs, frustrated.*)

What, doesn't it?

JOAN. No.

THOMAS. No?

JOAN. No! I hear that so often but, I think it's lazy! And not true. *I've* never felt it. I mean, a sky full of stars? Makes me feel big. So big I could *burst* out of my chest, I /..

THOMAS. Go on.

JOAN. It's, it's like, the bigness up there, the expanse, the vast possibilities, responds to the same in me. In you. There's a whole sky inside of you! I wish we'd all remember that. And if only *they* could see it! Then we'd all be free, praise God.

THOMAS. You always give the glory to God /

JOAN. Always.

THOMAS. And yet it's you that's done the work? You speak
of God *so lovingly*! And, I don't understand?! I can
barely even say the word without cringing. God. /..
God, Jesus, Church, I /.. If I'm truly honest, I've never
felt at home in a Church. I know I'm supposed to but
/.. In truth I'm baffled! Can't get my head 'round it all
and, and match *that* with what I feel in my heart I /..
In truth I fear I may have lost my faith forever. Maybe,
maybe never even had it? Which, *cuts, me, off*, from
everyone everywhere I, to live a Godless life is, it's
lonely and /.. But then *you* come along?! And I relate
to you *so much* you, you have no idea! You, you excite
and, *inspire*, and *wake me up*! And I ask you how you
are capable of doing this, *how*?! You're poor and young
like me! And, and then female too?! How are you so
brave?!

JOAN. By the grace of God.

THOMAS. Explain that, please! I /.. This God of yours, it's
found in a Church?

JOAN. Sometimes.

THOMAS. Sometimes?!

JOAN. Rarely. More often, *out*, with the clouds and the
trees and the people. Church is but *one* house for God,
Thomas, there are many.

THOMAS. You'd better not let them hear you speak this
way. You'll be killed for such a God.

JOAN. In time, yes.

THOMAS. And yet you remain faithful? The way you speak
of it, the smile it forms? It seems so confident and,
energizing? Like it brings you great comfort?

JOAN. It does.

THOMAS. Yet those men?! They make it so difficult for you, to be you and /.. *How* are you so brave?!

JOAN. By the grace of God. She is the fuel, without Her I'm nothing /

THOMAS. She?!

JOAN. Of course!

THOMAS. I apologise, I never meant to offend you!

JOAN. You haven't. It's about Love, Thomas. Those who live in Love live in God. You believe in love? You wish to love, and be loved /

THOMAS. Of course.

JOAN. Of course! It's the fabric of our existence. So, we follow what's loving. What's honest? What's true?

> (**THOMAS** *looks up to the sky and shyly crosses his chest.* **JOAN** *holds his chin, directs it back down.*)

Not up there.

> (**JOAN** *places one of his hands on his heart, and the other on his belly.*)

Here.

> (**THOMAS** *smiles, nods. He stands, ready to leave, turns back to* **JOAN**.)

THOMAS. Give people time to catch up with you.

JOAN. I fear they never will.

THOMAS. They will, in time, you'll see. Love is patient.

> (**JOAN** *nods.* **THOMAS** *exits.* **JOAN** *sits alone, meditates. Dawn rises.*)

Scene Four

(**SOLDIER ONE** *bursts in, waking everyone up.*)

SOLDIER ONE. Sir! Sir!

DUNOIS. What is it?

SOLDIER ONE. The people sir! The citizens of Orléans! They've been waiting for Joan to return, and now she has, they have raised arms!

SOLDIER TWO. What?

SOLDIER ONE. An urban militia! A new army! Inspired by Joan!

(*Everyone stares at* **JOAN,** *who looks stunned.*)

JOAN. *(To* **THOMAS.***)* You were right!

DUNOIS. What?!

THOMAS. Nothing!

SOLDIER THREE. They'll wake the English! Our plan is ruined!

SOLDIER TWO. Sir? What are our orders?

DUNOIS. *(To* **SOLDIERS TWO** *and* **THREE.***)* Wake the men!

(**SOLDIERS TWO** *and* **THREE** *run off.* **JOAN** *is already pumped up and pulling on armour.*)

JOAN. It is a sign! It is a sign from God! It's time to fight!

DUNOIS. No! No wait! We must have a strategy! We must plan!

JOAN. We need no strategy, we have the people! We are fueled by God! By the Love of France!

SOLDIER ONE. *(Passing* **DUNOIS** *a telescope.)* They're at the inner gates sir!

DUNOIS. What?

SOLDIER ONE. Armed with whatever they can find, ready to fight, cheering for Joan!

DUNOIS. Idiots! They know not what they do!

SOLDIER ONE. They're banging on the gates sir! Demanding to fight!

JOAN. Then let them!

DUNOIS. No! A thousand people with kitchen knives and enthusiasm? It'll be chaos!

SOLDIER ONE. They're not trained!

JOAN. They need no training!

SOLDIER ONE. They're just ordinary people, common people!

DUNOIS. It's not safe! *We* are professional commanders! We must guide them /

JOAN. I am ordinary! I am common! I will fight, *with* the people, *for* the people!

DUNOIS. No /

JOAN. I will fight, with or without you!

      *(***SOLDIER TWO** *runs in.)*

SOLDIER TWO. Sir! The militia have burst through the inner gates!

DUNOIS. What?

      *(***SOLDIER TWO** *points.* **DUNOIS** *looks through the telescope.)*

SOLDIER TWO. They're running towards the garrison! The English are so shocked they've not fired at them yet.

SOLDIER ONE. But no doubt they will! Archers all along the city walls.

DUNOIS. They're raising their bows, ready to fire down on them! Fuck! *(To* **SOLDIER ONE.***)* Get me my armour!

(**SOLDIER ONE** *runs off.*)

SOLDIER TWO. There's even women! And children! With pitchforks and broom handles!

DUNOIS. Fucking 'ell!

JOAN. But this is brilliant! If they take the garrison from the inside then they're providing us with an opening?

DUNOIS. They'll be lucky to survive it! They're civilians, pushing against trained soldiers!

SOLDIER TWO. Even if they did break through, how would we manage them? How will they know who to fight?

DUNOIS. It'll be chaos!

(**SOLDIER ONE** *returns with armour for* **DUNOIS. JOAN** *grabs the telescope off* **DUNOIS.***)*

SOLDIER ONE. They're wild sir! Calling for Joan!

JOAN. Tell them to prepare. I am coming for them!

DUNOIS. No! Fucksake! Wait! It's not safe! This is *not* how things are done!

JOAN. It is today!

(**SOLDIER THREE** *bursts in. The drums build.*)

SOLDIER THREE. Sir! The militia are attacking the garrison from the inside!

SOLDIER ONE. Oh God! Oh God!

SOLDIER TWO. What are our orders?

JOAN. Join them! Attack the garrison!

DUNOIS. No!

JOAN. Cross the river! To victory!

SOLDIER THREE. How?! There's no bridge!

SOLDIER ONE. They burned it!

JOAN. We'll make one! Attack! I command it!

DUNOIS. I am the commander here! *I* am the commander here! My name is Jean de Dunois. I have over *thirty* years experience at war, and I will *not* take orders from a /

JOAN. Do you want to win the war or be the man who won it? Is your focus the liberation of France or the celebration of your name?

DUNOIS. How dare you speak to me like that? So boldly?!

JOAN. And yet I wasn't finished /

DUNOIS. More words than should be possible for a woman to speak /

JOAN. More words will I speak sir, and louder too if you insist on interrupting!

DUNOIS. I'm unclear madam, if your persistence is the product of insanity or stupidity /

JOAN. Neither! It is the will of God /

DUNOIS. But either way the solution is silence!

JOAN. I will speak!

DUNOIS. I will remove you!

THOMAS. Sir, please! I might suggest you calm /

DUNOIS. I *am* calm /

THOMAS. I can see that /

JOAN. I will speak /

SOLDIER THREE. This is insanity /

JOAN. Hear me!

DUNOIS. Get her out /

SOLDIER ONE. Sir /

JOAN. Hear me /

SOLDIER TWO. Sir /

JOAN. Hear me now! I promise, with every drop of blood in this body, the future history books will bear my name! I'll make it so. Make it impossible not to!

DUNOIS. Get her out of here! Now!

JOAN. Men *will* write about me! And little girls many hundreds of years from today will study me in books. My strength will travel the ages, through the pages she holds. She'll read my words and feel power! Even for just a moment /

DUNOIS. Right, I'll bloody remove her myself then!

THOMAS. *(Physically blocking him.)* Sir, I must insist you calm /

JOAN. Men *will* write about me! *(Suddenly rooted, granite truth, fast and furious.)* And no doubt incorrectly. So comfortable writing as men, about men, for other men, these men will cringe and frown at the letters of my name. Grumble their way through scribing my success. Call it a fluke. Call me a freak. Stamp on my grave. For make no mistake I *will* be killed for my courage. Though the source of that be Divine, believe me, I'm incapable of being so brave. My natural disposition, feminine and frail, as taught by all who came before couldn't *possibly* have me on my feet, fighting for France?! And yet, here we are! And here I am! The reluctant messenger, the impossible soldier, God's warrior. Joan!

DUNOIS. Enough! That's enough! My patience is worn thin /

JOAN. If you won't hear me I will speak to the people directly.

DUNOIS. No you won't!

JOAN. I'll address those who *truly* matter!

DUNOIS. You'll do as you're told!

SOLDIER ONE. Sir /

JOAN. Let me speak /

DUNOIS. Shut up!

SOLDIER TWO. Sir /

JOAN. Let me *speak* /

DUNOIS. No!

JOAN. No?! No. How familiar that word is to me. Two tiny letters, yet such weight.

> (**JOAN** *suddenly climbs out of* **DUNOIS'** *reach.* **JOAN** *calls out across the river to address the militia.*)

Citizens of Orléans! I am here to lead you!

SOLDIER THREE. Good God!

DUNOIS. Stop her!

JOAN. These men say *no* to us, again and again!

SOLDIER THREE. She'll cause a riot!

DUNOIS. Get up there and stop her!

JOAN. No no no, over and over! For you, for anyone here for whom that exhausting word is familiar. If your ears are intricately intimate with the sound of *no*, to you I'm saying *yes*. I'm shouting *yes*, I'm screaming *yes* for you! Yes you can, yes you will, yes you /

DUNOIS. Get down, or I swear to God!

SOLDIER ONE. Sir! The citizens are climbing the garrison!

SOLDIER THREE. No! They'll be shot!

SOLDIER TWO. Our men are eager to join them!

SOLDIER THREE. What are our orders?

DUNOIS. Hold your positions! Hold!

JOAN. There is a voice, deep down inside every single one of us! Somehow we forgot? But it is there, still, it's there for you!

SOLDIER TWO. Sir! Our men are growing impatient!

SOLDIER THREE. We're losing control!

DUNOIS. Get her down! Stop her!

JOAN. Oh if we can just quiet the World for a moment! And listen within. There's a voice guiding you, I promise it's there. It's yours, and yours alone /

THOMAS. Joan /

DUNOIS. Get down /

JOAN. And until you can hear it, I'll *be* it for you!

THOMAS. Joan!

JOAN. And if you've lost faith, you can borrow my God. She's big enough for the both of us!

> *(A drummer enters the space, playing a solo.* **JOAN** *smiles at them.* **JOAN** *starts bouncing on the balls of their feet, fizzing up with power.* **DUNOIS** *stares.)*

DUNOIS. *(To* **JOAN**.*)* Stop! Stop that! *(To the drummer.)* Stop!

> *(***SOLDIER ONE***'s body starts being infected by* **JOAN**'s *power, shuddering, bouncing on his toes. He looks down at himself, surprised, tries to stop it, but can't. He looks up at* **DUNOIS**, *who is staring, in awe of it.)*

SOLDIER ONE. Sir?!

DUNOIS. Stop it! Stop that!

SOLDIER ONE. I can't sir!

SOLDIER THREE. Sir, the English archers have started firing!

SOLDIER TWO. Our men are ready to attack!

DUNOIS. No, we must prepare! We must /

> (**SOLDIER TWO**'s *body starts shuddering too.*
> **DUNOIS** *sees the power.*)

Good God!

SOLDIER TWO. *(Looking at his own body.)* Sir?! Sir!

SOLDIER THREE. Sir? What are our orders?

DUNOIS. Hold!

> (**SOLDIER THREE**'s *body begins shuddering
> too. Another drummer enters.* **DUNOIS** *sees it
> and spins on the spot, confused.*)

Hold your positions! Until we are clear on /

> (*Another drummer enters. The shudder in
> the* **MEN**'s *bodies builds, their arms slowly
> raising to the sky.* **DUNOIS** *spins and spins.*)

No! No wait! WAIT!

SOLDIER THREE. SIR?!

JOAN. RAISE YOUR SWORD!

DUNOIS. NO! HOLD YOUR POSITIONS!

JOAN. LET ME LEAD THEM!

DUNOIS. NO!

> (*Drums build.*)

JOAN. THEY ARE READY FOR ME! THEY *WANT* ME
TO LEAD THEM!

DUNOIS. NO!

SOLDIER ONE. SIR! OUR MEN HAVE RAISED ARMS!

DUNOIS. NO! WAIT! WAIT!

> *(Drums build.)*

SOLDIER ONE. SIR?!

SOLDIER TWO. SIR?!

DUNOIS. HOLD YOUR POSITIONS!

> *(Drums build.)*

JOAN. LET ME LEAD THEM!

SOLDIER ONE. SIR?!

DUNOIS. HOLD THEM BACK!

JOAN. LET ME LEAD THEM!

DUNOIS. NO!

> *(**JOAN** roars! Head tipped back, in alignment,*
> *power coursing through them. Huge!*
> *Transcendental! The **MEN** shuddering,*
> *their hands in the air, eyes to the sky. Then,*
> *suddenly, **JOAN** and the drums stop. The **MEN***
> *freeze. **JOAN** snaps their head to **DUNOIS.**)*

JOAN. *(Quietly.)* Follow me. In the name of God, follow
me.

Scene Five

(Boom! Everything explodes! Everyone's bodies shudder and shake, power bursting out of them, arms and legs thrashing violently. **JOAN** *leads the war-dance, and the* **MEN** *copy.)*

*(***JOAN*** summons more* **DANCERS** *from the crowd. Young, female-bodied, and queer* **DANCERS.** *Appearing from nowhere, and everywhere, drawn from the earth by* **JOAN***'s power.* **JOAN** *summons them, like a DJ sorcerer, infecting and bewitching, they're under a spell. The* **DANCERS** *move towards* **JOAN** *like they're possessed, like they're being electrocuted with pleasure and power, adrenaline surging through their bodies. Bodies full of swagger and sex and violence. They move through the yard to the front of the stage. The pressure between the* **MEN** *onstage and the* **AFAB DANCERS** *in the yard builds and builds and builds.* **DUNOIS** *stops moving suddenly, shocked by the* **AFAB DANCERS.** **DUNOIS** *and* **JOAN** *lock eyes.* **DUNOIS** *agrees and signals to the* **MEN.** *The* **MEN** *shift their positions to allow room for the* **AFAB DANCERS,** *who climb up onto the stage. They turn to face us, and all move together. Suddenly,* **JOAN** *has their* **ARMY.***)*

(Together they fight the English and drive them out of Orléans, in a war-dance that's organised chaos. It's a rave and a riot. Raw and honest. Sometimes a clump of bodies, sometimes weaving in and out of each other, sometimes in formation, sometimes bursting across the stage. Manic wild chaos, then suddenly they're miraculously in sync again.

Military drums and repetitive strings, over and over and over, looping and looping. Hypnotic and weird. It's breathtaking to watch. We completely forget to breathe, hearts in our chests, full of adrenaline. It makes you want to run or fight or fuck or dance or smash or something. Makes you feel animal. Makes you feel really human. Makes you feel fucking alive, so alive and powerful. Like we've suddenly remembered that we have access to the infinite, that it courses through our bodies like blood like sound like electricity like fire like fuck! **JOAN**, *like the rockstar we've always wanted, finds a megaphone and screams into it.)*

JOAN. WE ARE GOD'S WARRIORS! WE ARE THE MIGHTY! WE ARE FUELED BY GOD!

*(***JOAN'S ARMY*** dances, hard! Strong back, eyes ahead, head up, strutting forwards, one big step at a time. Their arms going crazy searching for something in the air or drumming or thrashing, like their skin is on fire. It's strength and fluid and sex and muscle and bone. It jumps between looking like a rave, to looking like a personal expression of oh-my-god-look-how-magic-my-body-is, to elegant mediaeval choreography, to violent thrashing and bouncing, to simple cheeky pedestrian gestures that ooze swagger. Sometimes they're enjoying themselves, we see it on their faces, they feel fucking sexy and they know they look fucking cool. Sometimes it's almost like they're a bit scared of their own power, in awe of it coursing through their human bodies. Sometimes they obey* **JOAN** *in their command of choreography with military precision. Sometimes they seem*

*possessed, their faces emotionless, their bodies
performing incredible feats of endurance and
talent. A searching hunger for God. A physical
thirst for God. A physical celebration of God.
A physical surrendering to God. A physical
manifestation of God.)*

JOAN.   WE ARE GOD'S WARRIORS! WE ARE THE
MIGHTY! WE ARE FUELED BY GOD!

ALL.   WE ARE GOD'S WARRIORS! WE ARE THE
MIGHTY! WE ARE FUELED BY GOD!

JOAN.   FOLLOW ME! FOLLOW ME! IF YOU LOVE ME
FOLLOW ME!

*(***JOAN'S ARMY*** pushes forward, together. The
attack is bloody and brilliant. It's electric. It's
punk. It's passion. It's biblical. It's vibrant.
It's brutal. It's dark. It's terrifying and
wonderful and epic and sexy it's sex it's pure
fucking sex it's sweaty human bodies that
seem so animal oh god we are all so animal
and pretending to be human.* **JOAN** *is swept
up in the energy and climbs high, higher,
higher, dangerously high, and cries out in
ecstasy.)*

AU NOM DE DIEU!

(And in that moment of total openness, **JOAN**
*is hit with an arrow to the shoulder. Time
slows, weirdly suspended. Sudden grace,
sudden softness, elegance and eloquence.
Fluid delicate bodies making sweeping
shapes in the air, caught in the breeze,
twirling and suspended for longer than
should seem possible. Then* **JOAN** *falls. And
there's horrible silence and stillness. The* **MEN**
rush to **JOAN***'s side.* **JOAN** *looks dead. Then,
impossibly,* **JOAN** *wakes.)*

THOMAS. Joan! Lie still! Call for the doctor! The doctor! Now!

DUNOIS. That'll take days! You! Get bandages and some alcohol, quickly! We must stop the bleeding.

JOAN. No! There's no time!

DUNOIS. You'll be all right kid. We'll find a surgeon later.

JOAN. No, there's no *time*! We must push forward!

> (**JOAN** *puts their hand around the arrow and takes a deep breath.*)

DUNOIS. NO!

> (**JOAN** *cries out as they pull the arrow from their own shoulder.* **JOAN** *drags themself upwards and stands, swaying. The* **MEN** *stare in awe.*)

JOAN. Forward. Forward!

> (**JOAN** *leads the dance again. It builds and builds and builds. The* **DANCERS** *start killing each other, and killing themselves, in many various ways, and then getting back up off the floor, and repeating. It's an endless killing loop that is horrible and hilarious.* **JOAN** *finds the megaphone again.*)

WE ARE FUELED BY GOD! GOD'S POWER IS *IN* US! IT POURS *THROUGH* US! CAN YOU FEEL IT?! *CAN YOU FEEL IT?!* I AM FULL OF GOD! I AM FULL OF GOD! *I AM FULL OF GOD!*

ALL. I AM FULL OF GOD! I AM FULL OF GOD! I AM FULL OF GOD!

JOAN. WE ARE THE MIGHTY! WE ARE THE MIGHTY!

> (*The phrases "I am full of God" and "We are the mighty" loop and twist and turn.*

Hypnotic and weird and frightening. Drums and drums and drums. The killing loop repeats over and over. The war-dance builds, bodies throb in fury. One **DANCER** *suddenly stops, looks out, her eyes shining. She points.)*

DANCER TWO. They flee! They flee! We are victorious!

Scene Six

(Everyone cheers. They're exhausted. The drumming subsides as the adrenaline calms. **JOAN** *keeps thrashing and thrashing and thrashing.)*

JOAN. We are the mighty! We are the mighty, we are the, we are, the mighty the, the mighty, the /

(Someone finds a way to put a hand on **JOAN***'s shoulder.* **JOAN** *stills, sways, catches their breath.* **JOAN** *comes back to earth and sees the truth. Is horrified by the gore of war.)*

The mighty the, the mighty, fallen? ...No. No, no this cannot be right? This cannot be right?!

DUNOIS. Joan! I owe you an apology. I stand corrected. Completely corrected. I mean, bloody 'eck! You kid, you're a marvel! Honestly I /.. I must say, it was an honour to serve with you. Truly, an honour. I honestly /

JOAN. No! No this, this cannot be, this cannot be!

THOMAS. Joan? What's wrong?

JOAN. This! *This!*

DUNOIS. *(To* **THOMAS.***)* It's okay. *(Pulling* **JOAN** *aside.)* Joan, hey, look at me, look at me. Breathe. Breathe, you're all right, you're all right! Just, breathe, kid. That's it. That's it, let it pass through yer.

*(***JOAN** *tries to follow* **DUNOIS'** *instruction, but is wild with energy.)*

JOAN. What have we done? What have we done?!

DUNOIS. Our duty. And we've done so brilliantly! You're brilliant! Listen, what you did today, was incredible. Truly, incredible.

JOAN. It's awful! This is awful!

DUNOIS. *(Gently.)* This is war, Joan. It's brutal. The worst of humanity. No matter how much we advance as a species like, we always seem to come back to this. It's barbaric. But I guess, ultimately, humans will always be fighting. We can't all be peacekeepers forever. Someone will always pick up a sword eventually, and if you don't kill you'll be killed, it's as simple as that. But you were brave today, kid. You got right down in the mud and the blood with us didn't yer?! And I commend you for that, I really do. Because most commanders would rather not fight, given the choice. Oh no, they'd much prefer to push paper 'round. Forget that these men are in fact men. They're somebody's brother, or husband, or son. Not some statistic, not a number. They're men, *my* men, it's *my* job to take care of 'em. I'd die for any of them. And you. I'd die for you now too kid. My sword and shield are in your hands.

> *(**DUNOIS** holds out his hand. **JOAN** shakes it. Then **JOAN** catches sight of a **SOLDIER** about to kill a **WOUNDED SOLDIER**.)*

JOAN. Stop! *Stop!* What are you *doing*?!

SOLDIER THREE. He's English /

JOAN. No! No needless killing! The siege has been raised, is that not enough?! The ground is soaked with blood, is that not enough?! Is that not enough?!

> *(The **SOLDIERS** stare at **JOAN**, who weaves through bits of bloodied bodies. **JOAN** turns to us and speaks to God.)*

Oh God! Oh God please! Please help me to breathe. I /.. I can't calm down I can't calm down I, I'm shaking I /.. Body feels like it's on fire! /.. What am I doing? What the hell am I doing? Is this the right thing?! What's this for, who's this all for?

*(**CHARLES** enters, full of beans. The **SOLDIERS** try to find the energy to bow for him.)*

CHARLES. Fantastic! *Fantastic!* Congratulations men! *Yes!* Congratulations Joan! *Fantastic!*

JOAN. .

CHARLES. Now then, look about you! Come, come there is more to be done!

JOAN. *(Quietly.)* More?

CHARLES. We must advance! *Immediately!* The campaign starts today! Just as Joan suggested, we'll take each city by force! Battle by bloody battle, all the way to Reims, and my coronation! Hurrah!

DANCERS & SOLDIERS. *(Exhausted.)* Hurrah!

JOAN. No! Oh my God, no!

> *(Everyone stares at **JOAN**, who looks to **DUNOIS**, lost. **CHARLES** sees. **DUNOIS** nods at **JOAN**.)*

DUNOIS. You're all right kid. My sword and shield.

> *(**DUNOIS** turns to everyone.)*

Come gentlemen, and ladies. Our new army! Come everyone, to arms!

> *(The **SOLDIERS** and **DANCERS** get on their bellies and drag their tired bodies slowly upstage. **CHARLES** pulls **JOAN** downstage.)*

CHARLES. Joan! What's wrong? You were magnificent, a true warrior!

JOAN. Sir, please! Please! We must stop! I /.. I cannot go on!

CHARLES. You can! Oh Joan you can, and you must!

JOAN. No!

CHARLES. Your country needs you! God, *God* has called you to war! I didn't quite believe it at first, but I know now. I've seen it with my own eyes. You are a wonder, Joan, truly! The only word for it, is a *miracle*!

JOAN. No, no sir I /

CHARLES. And I needed a miracle! Oh, I was so lost! I'd truly lost faith in everything. You know, secretly, I'd always *hoped* I was capable of Greatness. Called to be something Great? And yet. /.. And then you arrived. A nobody from nowhere. The most unlikely hero man's ever seen, and yet the hero we all needed, I needed, I need you Joan.

JOAN. It's awful! Awful, bloody /

CHARLES. Yes, it is! So awful. But a means to an end! A beautiful end! Justice is worth fighting for. Joan, you told me I would be King, you told me we'd win the war, you told me this was God's will for us.

JOAN. Yes! But I can't do it *again*! The cost is *so high*! And the task ahead is *huge*, it's enormous it's I, I cannot go on I cannot /

CHARLES. *(Quietly and firmly.)* You can, and you must, Joan. You *must*!

JOAN. *(Quietly.)* I am afraid.

CHARLES. As am I! And yet, God calls us to be brave, so brave we shall be. Together. Joan, I need you.

> *(**JOAN** agrees. **CHARLES** is relieved.)*

Tell me again. City by city, battle by bloody battle /

JOAN. Liberation by liberation /

CHARLES. Yes /

JOAN. All the way to Reims /

CHARLES. And my coronation.

JOAN. Yes. Then *straight* on to Paris. Once we have the capital /

CHARLES. We'll easily take Rouen.

JOAN. Yes. Then we shall drive the English into the sea! Liberate France! Freedom!

CHARLES. Yes!

JOAN. A *new* freedom, *for* the people, *by* the people! Free from English church and state.

CHARLES. Yes!

JOAN. Free to live and love and worship as they will! We shall free them at last!

CHARLES. Yes!

Together we shall!

JOAN. Together.

>   (**CHARLES** *turns to* **JOAN'S ARMY**, *who is stood in formation upstage.*)

CHARLES. ONWARDS!

Scene Seven

(A trumpet sounds, and the **MEN** *cross the stage in formation, led by* **JOAN**. **CHARLES** *is ushered into the centre of them, protected by their bodies.* **JOAN'S ARMY** *fight-dances their way across the space.* **CHARLES** *whimpers and watches as they battle, bloody and brilliant, in his honour. One difficult challenge after another, they climb the ladder of success.* **JOAN** *is spectacular, this incredible queer icon we've all been waiting for.)*

JOAN. Strike hard! And the English will retreat! In God's name!

ALL. Amen!

SOLDIER ONE. *(Pointing ahead.)* Saint-Florentin?

JOAN. Taken!

(**JOAN'S ARMY** *cheers.)*

Onwards!

(**JOAN'S ARMY** *focuses again, moving together as one unit.)*

SOLDIER ONE. *(Pointing ahead.)* Saint-Fargeau?

JOAN. Taken!

(**JOAN'S ARMY** *cheers.)*

Onwards!

(**JOAN'S ARMY** *focuses again. The* **DANCERS** *pop out to call to* **JOAN**.)

DANCER ONE. Joan?

JOAN. Are you all right? Do you have everything you need?

DANCER TWO. Yes yes, we're fine! Thank you!

JOAN. Are the men respecting you?

DANCER ONE. Oh we've dealt with worse! We can handle a few stubborn men!

JOAN. Of course! You are the strongest women I know. The silent survivors of war, the unsung heroes! Men won't write about you, but I know you are the bones of this movement, this Great Change! From the bottom of my heart, I thank you for your service.

DANCER TWO. We thank *you*!

DANCER ONE. For inspiring it! After all these years?! And all these men, with their broken promises /

DANCER TWO. And their lies /

DANCER ONE. And their *endless* fighting /

DANCER TWO. Again and again and again?! I, I couldn't go on much longer I /.. We *needed* change, *I* needed, desperate, drastic change!

DANCER ONE. A revolution!

DANCER TWO. Yes!

DANCER ONE. And there you are! The answer to all our prayers!

JOAN. *You* are the answer! You have such grit! And such grace! God is *within* you. Don't ever forget that.

SOLDIER ONE. Joan? *(Pointing ahead.)* Brienon-sur-Armançon?

JOAN. Taken!

     *(**JOAN'S ARMY** cheers.)*

Onwards!

     *(**JOAN** rejoins the throb of bodies. **THOMAS** pops out to join the **DANCERS**.)*

DANCER ONE. Our army is growing each day!

THOMAS. I can't believe it!

DANCER TWO. People travel from all over! On ponies, with
pitchforks /

THOMAS. Ponies?!

DANCER TWO. On hand and foot if they must, all in the
name of Joan!

SOLDIER ONE. *(Pointing ahead.)* Auxerre?

JOAN. Taken!

(**JOAN'S ARMY** *cheers.*)

Onwards!

DANCER ONE. She humiliates the English!

DANCER TWO. They're panicked! Horrified! Claiming a
sorceress has saved France!

THOMAS. They are being massacred, town by town /

SOLDIER ONE. *(Pointing.)* Champagne, Troyes, Châlons-
sur-Marne?!

JOAN. Taken! Taken! Taken!

(**JOAN'S ARMY** *cheers.*)

Onwards!

(**THOMAS** *disappears into the mass of bodies.*
SOLDIERS TWO *and* **THREE** *pop out.*)

SOLDIER TWO. Joan is *furious* in her attack, fierce!

DANCER TWO. She's like a captain of twenty /

SOLDIER THREE. *Thirty* years experience!

DANCER ONE. Fearless on the battlefield!

SOLDIER TWO. You're pretty fearless too!

SOLDIER THREE. Yeah I must say I've been impressed by you lot!

DANCER ONE. Well don't underestimate us!

SOLDIER TWO. Together we are stronger!

DANCERS ONE & TWO & SOLDIER THREE. Together!

JOAN. Onwards!

> (**JOAN'S ARMY** *cheers. The* **SOLDIERS** *disappear into the mass of bodies, and the* **AFAB DANCERS** *pop out.*)

DANCER FIVE. She inspires me!

ALL DANCERS. And me!

DANCER ONE. Makes me feel alive! For the first time since my husband was killed, I feel alive again, awake! Like I have so much to do, so much to give!

DANCER TWO. Yes! She makes me believe I could do more with my life. When the war is over /

DANCER FOUR. If it's *ever* over /

DANCER TWO. Then maybe I don't have to just stay at home, and cook and clean and /.. I could do more? I'm suddenly seeing that! The world is really big!

ALL DANCERS. Yes!

DANCER THREE. She is, the most incredible example of God!

DANCER FOUR. Yes, but not, boring, church God /

DANCER THREE. No!

DANCER FOUR. New, fresh, yes yes, oh my god yes God!

ALL DANCERS. Yes!

DANCER ONE. This new power!

DANCER FOUR. This vibrant being!

DANCER THREE. Oh the vibrancy!

DANCER ONE. She gives me goosebumps just looking at her!

DANCER TWO. Me too! She is *so* beautiful!

DANCER FIVE. She's sexy. Dare I say it?

ALL DANCERS. Yes!

DANCER TWO. So fierce, and so strong!

DANCER FOUR. Winning battle after *impossible* battle!

DANCER THREE. Leading us to victory!

DANCER FIVE. Yes! I actually think we're going to win the war?!

ALL DANCERS. Yes!

DANCER THREE. Yes I believe it!

DANCER FIVE. She makes me believe /

DANCER ONE. Makes me believe in some kind of God again /

DANCER TWO. Makes me feel like God believes in me!

JOAN. Onwards!

> (**JOAN'S ARMY** *cheers.*)

Follow me! Follow me! If you love me, follow me!

> (**JOAN** *is surrounded by their* **ARMY**, *moving together, supporting and celebrating each other. Together they are strong, a queer and female force to be reckoned with. There's laughter too, it looks fun to be them.* **CHARLES** *watches, jealous.* **YOLANDE** *and* **MARIE** *appear from nowhere.*)

MARIE. Charles darling? Why are you sulking?

CHARLES. I'm not! …It's just, oh look! The people *love* her!

MARIE. They love *you* for whom she serves!

CHARLES. You think so?

MARIE. Of course!

CHARLES. Yes, yes she's innocent! Everyone tells me so.

YOLANDE. Even the innocent can be seduced by power. However, I believe there to be no cause for concern here. She's a child.

MARIE. And proving very useful to us.

> (**CHARLES** *nods, watching* **JOAN**. **JOAN** *smiles and waves at the trio. They perform a big cheery wave back.*)

YOLANDE. We are *almost* there. After all these years, the crown is *within reach*!

CHARLES. Yes!

YOLANDE. So focus, Charles, *focus*!

CHARLES. Yes.

MARIE. Yes, try not to lose your head darling.

> (*The* **SOLDIERS** *join the* **DANCERS**, *having fun dancing together. They start getting raucous, joy spilling out their skin, all over* **JOAN**. **DUNOIS** *appears.*)

DUNOIS. Come on men! *And* women! Our new army! As you know I had my doubts, but the militia have proved me wrong. We are fighting *together* and we are stronger for it!

> (*Everyone cheers.*)

Now listen, we've done incredibly to get this far. But the task ahead will be challenging, to say the least. We have one final push to get into Reims! We need to rest and refuel the horses, repair the wagons, sharpen the blades, restock our weaponry. And all as quickly as possible, as we know our Joan won't hang about. We are almost there lads! Are you with me?

(Everyone cheers.)

Away with yer then!

(Everyone scatters to do their various jobs. The stage is full of people, hurrying in and out, on various journeys across the space. **JOAN** *starts taking big boxes of military equipment off a wagon.* **THOMAS** *appears and helps. They speak as they work.)*

THOMAS. Madam? How are you feeling?

JOAN. Fine! I'm fine! Thank you... But Thomas, must we persist with these constant *madams*?

THOMAS. It is polite, is it not?

JOAN. It may be, but /..

THOMAS. But what?

JOAN. Oh I /.. I don't know.

*(***SOLDIER ONE*** appears with armfulls of armour.)*

(To **SOLDIER ONE.***)* Yes, very good!

*(***JOAN*** points, and* **SOLDIER ONE*** exits that way.* **JOAN*** turns back to* **THOMAS.***)*

Do you ever feel like, sometimes, the words we have, aren't good enough? I speak them, and as soon as my mouth forms the sound I, I must admit I'm disappointed.

> *(DANCER TWO, DANCER THREE and SOLDIER*
> *TWO cross the stage with equipment, working*
> *together happily.)*

A world of words on my tongue and yet, sometimes *(To* **SOLDIER THREE** *appearing.)* Yes! Very good! Onwards!

SOLDIER THREE. Onwards!

> *(SOLDIER THREE exits. SOLDIER ONE and*
> *DANCER ONE cross the stage carrying a big*
> *box between them.)*

JOAN. Love, for example, love. L. O /

THOMAS. V. E.

JOAN. Four *tiny* letters, for such a *huge* thing?!

THOMAS. Ha! Yes!

JOAN. Should the word not be *longer*? More /

THOMAS. Complicated?

JOAN. Yes! A challenge to articulate. I almost spit it out. Love. Love. *(To* **SOLDIER ONE** *appearing.)* Love. Oh, sorry! Onwards!

SOLDIER ONE. Onwards!

> *(SOLDIER ONE exits. DANCERS FOUR and*
> *FIVE enter with equipment, and JOAN gestures*
> *to where it should go.)*

JOAN. Love. Life. Earth, sky, God! Why are all the big things such small words?!

THOMAS. I've never noticed!

> *(DANCERS TWO and THREE appear with fresh*
> *armour for JOAN.)*

JOAN. And then girl? Boy? Man, woman, they're not big enough are they?

THOMAS. In, length you mean?

> (*The* **DANCERS** *dress* **JOAN.**)

JOAN. That too but, not big enough in, in concept or /..
Not enough space for all of us to, fit, neatly inside, one
or the other. Does it not seem *strange* that *all* of us
must fit neatly into one or the other?

THOMAS. I suppose.

JOAN. Girl? Boy. Girl. Girl, ugh /..

THOMAS. I know it must be, frustrating, sometimes, to be
a woman.

DANCER ONE. No you don't.

THOMAS. No, I don't.

DANCER ONE. Understatement of the century!

DANCER TWO. Yeah but, there's beauty in it too. I *love*
being a woman.

DANCER ONE. Yeah, I wouldn't change it, even if I could.

JOAN. You wouldn't? Really?

BOTH DANCERS. No.

JOAN. That's wonderful you feel that way.

THOMAS. You don't?

> (**JOAN** *checks quickly that they're not being
> overheard.*)

JOAN. It's just it's, never felt like, the right word for me.

THOMAS. Woman?

> (**JOAN** *shakes their head, shyly.*)

JOAN. It's incorrect. Somehow. Despite this /..

(JOAN gestures to their body. THOMAS and the DANCERS are confused.)

I don't *feel* myself living inside the word. I try to lift my feet up, tuck myself in tight, twist here, squash there, bend out of shape to squeeze inside but /..

DANCER ONE. But?

JOAN. I don't fit.

DANCER TWO. I think you do fine.

JOAN. No, it's the wrong word. And yet, there *is* not a word, I am wordless! And it's *lonely*, not having language, worse it seems violent?! Who is it that chooses words?

THOMAS. Which?

JOAN. All of them? Who chooses the words for words? A man I presume?

THOMAS. Well, yes, probably. Maybe your word has just not been written yet?

JOAN. Maybe. I don't know, I can't even read!

(They laugh. SOLDIERS ONE and TWO burst in downstage. The rest of the ARMY get into formation upstage.)

SOLDIER TWO. Sir? We are ready to get back on the road!

SOLDIER ONE. Hourra!

SOLDIER TWO. The city of Reims lies ahead!

SOLDIER ONE. Where's Joan, is she ready?

JOAN. *(Quietly to themself.)* She.

(JOAN shudders. THOMAS sees.)

THOMAS. They will be soon. Thank you.

(The SOLDIERS nod and get into formation.)

JOAN. They.

> (**JOAN** *smiles at* **THOMAS.**)

THOMAS. Onwards, to Reims?

JOAN. ONWARDS!

> (**JOAN'S ARMY** *cheers.* **JOAN** *leads them as they move forward. We see a sped-up version of the last bit of the journey to Reims. They move in perfect sync, until* **JOAN** *suddenly cries out.*)

HOLD!

> (*They all pause, their bodies suspended. They look out and up slowly together. The task ahead looming. Everyone is suddenly shit scared.*)

SOLDIER TWO. Oh, my, God!

DANCER ONE. City walls! A hundred feet high?

SOLDIER ONE. A thousand, surely?!

SOLDIER THREE. Solid stone. How are we meant to get through that?!

DANCER TWO. Look at all those soldiers!

SOLDIER THREE. Soldiers? It's the archers I'm looking at!

SOLDIER TWO. We'll never make it!

SOLDIER ONE. It's impossible!

DANCER ONE. We'll be killed! We'll all be killed!

DUNOIS. QUIET!

> (*The* **ARMY** *falls silent.* **DUNOIS** *turns to* **JOAN.**)

(*Quietly.*) Joan, I hope to fuck you've got a plan kid?

CHARLES.   Joan! Joan! *(Pushing through the crowd, panicked.)* Joan! They'll never open the gates for me!

DUNOIS.   You what?

CHARLES.   They will *refuse* my coronation!

DUNOIS.   *(Quietly.)* Probably.

JOAN.   Never! You are the true King!

CHARLES.   They hate me!

JOAN.   They *love* you!

CHARLES.   They love *you* Joan! They love *you*!

JOAN.   Sir! Please! I know you are frightened /

CHARLES.   I'm not!

JOAN.   But have faith, all shall be well.

CHARLES.   All shall *not* be well! How can you say that? Your persistent optimism is infuriating, it's unbelievably infuriating!

DUNOIS.   Aye, that it can be.

CHARLES.   It's *offensive* in fact, yes, I am offended! You dare to tell me such *pretty* lies to bolster my hope, my *desperate* hope?! When in fact you ignore the basic truth, that I am doomed! Cursed! Illegitimate!

JOAN.   Sir! We *will* win this battle and the people *will* open the gates, I swear it! And you can take this victory as a sign from God, attesting to your Divine Legitimacy. You *are* the rightful King, soon to be crowned! *(Addressing everyone.)* The people want it so. Then as King you *shall* liberate France! Together we shall!

ALL.   Hourra!

CHARLES.   *(Still panicked.)* Right, yes, yes!

DUNOIS.   Aye, grand, but before then, what we gonna do about that? *(Pointing ahead.)* I don't mean to be the bearer of bad news like, but, I'm *all* out of ideas kid. That is a bloody big wall!

THOMAS. With *hundreds* of soldiers and archers! Thousands maybe? I have never seen so many troops protecting one city?!

DUNOIS. Nor me. We'd be *totally mad* to try and attack it!

JOAN. Attack it we will, and successfully!

DUNOIS. Right. Totally mad it is then?!

THOMAS. Oh God!

DUNOIS. Everyone, to arms!

DANCER ONE. What?!

SOLDIER THREE. No! This is impossible!

DANCER TWO. Oh, my, God?!

SOLDIER ONE. We're gonna die, we're all going to die?!

JOAN. *(To everyone.)* Have courage! Have, Courage! For I am fuelled by God! I will keep you safe! I will lead you to victory!

CHARLES. How?!

JOAN. I know the task ahead seems impossible /

SOLDIER TWO. Too right!

JOAN. But we have already achieved the impossible together, again and again! Look at us! *Look* at us! Never in our history have we had such a united army. We fight together, *for* the people, *by* the people! We fight as One, powered by Love, and that power is Infinite! We cannot fail! It'd be *impossible* for us to fail, for we are *fuelled by God*! A God that's *inside* each and every one of us, and strengthened by our unity! God is the fuel! We are *full* of God! We are full of God!

ALL. We are full of God! We are full of God!

(Their bodies shudder and shake, full of power.)

We are full of God! We are full of God! We are full of God!

JOAN. Yes! Now, focus! On my command!

(Their bodies shudder, the tension rising, like a wave about to crash.)

NOW!

(They burst forwards together, their bodies exploding. Fast and loud war-dance. They rave, hard, harder, harder still! Chanting "We Are Full Of God!" over and over until, with their fists in the air, they are roaring together, victorious!)

DUNOIS. WE DID IT!

CHARLES. OH MY GOD!

DUNOIS. OH MY FUCKING GOD! UNBELIEVABLE!

THOMAS. SIR! THE PEOPLE HAVE OPENED THE GATES!

CHARLES. OH MY GOD! JOAN?!

JOAN. GOD SAVE THE KING!

ALL. GOD SAVE THE KING! QUE DIEU SAUVE LE ROI!

*(Suddenly a voice soars out across the yard. Heavenly and beautiful, a hymn. Small pieces of white and gold cloth are attached to the **MEN**'s staffs, and hung down from above, so from a distance it looks like hundreds of birds or enormous butterflies hovering in the sunlight. The procession is beautiful. Everyone sings together quietly, a gorgeous*

choral number. **YOLANDE** *and* **MARIE** *watch*
as a **BISHOP** *stands before* **CHARLES.***)*

BISHOP. Monseigneur; accordez et soutenez-vous, et confirmez-vous par votre serment solennel, au Peuple de la France, les Lois, Obligations et Coutumes anciennes accordées au Clergé par votre Prédécesseur, selon les Lois de Dieu Tout-Puissant?

CHARLES. J'accorde et promets de le faire.

BISHOP. Soutenez-vous la Paix, et l'Accord Pieux, selon votre puissance et votre miséricorde, au Dieu, à la Sainte Église, à la clergie, et au Peuple de la France?

CHARLES. Je vous promets et vous accorde.

DANCER ONE. Jurez-vous de respecter la Justice et la Loi?

CHARLES. Je le jure solennellement.

BISHOP. De défendre et protéger la Sainte Église et la bonne volonté de sa Peuple?

CHARLES. Je le jure solennellement.

DANCER TWO. Do you swear to humbly serve the Good People of France? In particular, do you swear to defend and protect the poor, from all their adversaries?

CHARLES. To this I solemnly swear.

DANCER ONE. Jurez-vous de rendre service au bon Peuple de la France comme leur Seigneur souverain?

CHARLES. Je le jure solennellement.

BISHOP. Jurez-vous de défendre ce belle et noble patrie, et de conserver chacun de ses sujets?

CHARLES. Je le jure solennellement.

DANCER TWO. Jurez-vous de rendre service au Dieu Tout-Puissant, en tous vos paroles et vos actions?

CHARLES. Je le jure solennellement.

> (**CHARLES** *lays his hand upon the Bible.*)

Par mon cœur prêt et pieux, et par la grâce de Dieu Tout-Puissant, je vous en fais serment de faire tous que j'y sois jurer faire.

> (**CHARLES** *kisses the Bible and signs the Oath.*
> *The* **BISHOP** *and* **DANCERS** *turn out to us and*
> *address the house.*)

BISHOP. Dieu Tout-Puissant et Éternel, Créateur de tous, Roi des Rois et Seigneur des Seigneurs ! Écoutez, nous vous supplions, nos oraisons humbles et multipliez vos bénédictions sur ce votre serviteur Charles, qui en votre saint nom, avec dévotion et obéissance, nous sacrons notre véritable Souverain Roi.

DANCER ONE. Accordez-lui que par votre inspiration et votre bonté il puisse gouverner et prendre plaisir d'un Royaume paisible et bienheureuse. Accordez-lui par votre grâce qu'il puisse vous rendre service avec fierté et amour, et qu'il puisse se battre pour vous avec la fidèle constance.

DANCER TWO. Soutenez-lui par votre bras puissant. Entourer-lui par votre sauvegarde et patronage. Permettez-lui par votre vertu, de vaincre tous ses adversaires.

BISHOP. Honorez-lui au-dessus de tous les Rois de la terre. Permettez que la justice se resplendisse pendant son règne.

DANCER ONE. Accordez qu'il puisse régner avec Vous /

DANCER TWO. Qui est la voiec /

DANCER ONE. La vérité /

DANCER TWO. Et la vie /

DANCER ONE. En gloire dans votre Royaume par tous les siècles des siècles.

BISHOP. Par Jésus Christ notre Seigneur et Sauveur. Dieu, conservez notre Roi.

DANCERS & BISHOP. Amen.

> *(A **DANCER** approaches **CHARLES** with the crown. **CHARLES** signals that **JOAN** should crown him. **JOAN** is honoured. **JOAN** takes the crown from the **DANCER** and holds it high above their head for a moment longer than necessary, weirdly suspended. Everyone's heads lift up to look at the crown. The sun shines through the stained glass window, and **JOAN** is flooded in rainbow light. The crowd silently urges **JOAN** to put on the crown, and it looks for a moment like **JOAN** will. **YOLANDE** and **MARIE** snap their heads to each other, then back to **JOAN**. **JOAN** places the crown upon **CHARLES'** head.)*

JOAN. Que Dieu sauve le roi!

EVERYONE. Que Dieu sauve le roi!

> *(**JOAN** turns out to us, their eyes closed, singing. As soon as **JOAN** turns away the music changes, distorts, becomes remixed with something contemporary, something ugly. King **CHARLES** melts backwards into the crowd, partying, a blob of bodies gyrating over each other in a sexy messy hungry dirty blur of hedonism. The crowd slowly exits, taking the music with them. **JOAN** finishes singing a capella. **JOAN** opens their eyes, and realises they're alone, spins, afraid. **JOAN** looks at us, then runs offstage.)*

Interval

ACT II

Scene One

(*Loud music. Everyone bursts onstage and into their coronation positions. They dance, hard. It's a rave. Hedonistic and sweaty. We see some glimpses of the war-battle from before. But this is self indulgent, skin hungry for touch.* **JOAN** *suddenly appears in the middle of the chaos, holding the crown high above their head. They slowly lower it onto their own head, encouraged by the crowd.* **CHARLES** *suddenly snatches the crown.* **YOLANDE** *slaps* **JOAN** *across the face, and* **MARIE** *pushes* **JOAN** *downstage. Everyone turns their back on* **JOAN**. **CHARLES** *dances wildly with the crown on his head,* **YOLANDE** *and* **MARIE** *clapping him.* **JOAN** *tries to get to* **CHARLES**, *but a wall of dancing bodies stops them.* **JOAN** *looks at us, desperately spinning, then disappears. The music amps up and the dancing becomes more grotesque. The throb of bodies spits* **CHARLES** *out into the night. He is drunk and disgusting.*)

CHARLES. Fuck! Life is fucking sexy! I am fucking sexy! You are fucking sexy! Thomas! Thomas! Thomaaaaaaas?! Thomaaaaaaaas /

THOMAS. Yes sir?

CHARLES. Are you drunk?

THOMAS. Yes sir, a, a little, perhaps.

CHARLES. D'you feel sexy?

THOMAS. I /..

CHARLES. I want everyone to feel sexy!

THOMAS. Yes sir.

CHARLES. Do you?

THOMAS. I, I think so /

CHARLES. Think?! No! No don't *think*! You can't think and fuck at the same time Thomas. You're either in your head or in your body, and God knows you should be in your body. Look I'll show you! /.. There! I'm in my head. Ugh! Can you feel it?! It's so /.. Everything becomes so /.. And then look! /.. There! I'm back in my body! Can you feel that? /.. Feel that?!

THOMAS. Yes sir. I think I can feel that /

CHARLES. No no no! You're in your head again Thomas! No! I can see it on your face! It's /.. Ugh! It's fucking depressing! You need a fuck. No really, someone fuck Thomas! Someone fuck Thomas!

THOMAS. Oh no, please, I don't want /

CHARLES. Someone! Anyone?! Someone please, give this man a fuck!

THOMAS. No! Please, I really don't /

CHARLES. I command it, Thomas, as your King! As, your, King! Oh god I love saying that. *As, your, king!* Fuck I'm sexy! I am your sexy fucking King and I command you, to have a fucking good time!

THOMAS. Yes, it's just, there is much work to be done sir, and not much time. We should prepare our /

CHARLES. Careful! You sound just like Joan!

THOMAS. Well, I /

CHARLES. Rabbiting on about *not much time*? There's plenty of time when you're King!

THOMAS. Yes. Well, I just think /

CHARLES. No no no! Too many thoughts, not enough fucks! Stop *thinking*! Start *feeling*!

> (**CHARLES** *pulls* **DANCER TWO** *out of the throb of bodies.* **DANCER TWO** *wraps themself around* **THOMAS,** *who is stunned.*)

THOMAS. Oh! Oh I. /..

> (**THOMAS** *politely untangles himself from the* **DANCER.**)

Oh, no, no thank you.

> (**CHARLES** *laughs.*)

CHARLES. No! Not like that! Like this!

> (**CHARLES** *dances with* **DANCER TWO.** *The crowd cheers him on.* **CHARLES** *is embarrassing himself.* **THOMAS** *is disgusted and trying not to show it.* **MAN THREE** *enters and tries to get* **CHARLES'** *attention.*)

MAN THREE. Sir? Sir?

CHARLES. No! Not you! No! I forbid it! This is a party!

MAN THREE. But sir, it's Joan!

CHARLES. No! Jesus fuck! Can't you hear me? I SAID NO!

> (**MAN ONE** *and* **MAN TWO** *appear to watch.*)

MAN THREE. Yes sir, but it's just, she's very insistent!

CHARLES. I bet she fucking is!

MAN THREE. She says it's urgent!

CHARLES. Oh it's *always* urgent!

MAN THREE. She's been trying to contact you all day. All week in fact.

CHARLES. Yes, well, I've been busy, Very busy, doing King things because I am King!

(*Everyone cheers.*)

MAN ONE. Well said sir!

CHARLES. Thank you.

MAN TWO. Yes sir, you are well within your rights to turn anybody away.

MAN ONE. Yes of course.

MAN THREE. But, it's Joan /

CHARLES. *Fuck* Joan! All I hear is Joan! Joan Joan *Joan*! Joan *Joan Joan Joan Jooooaaaaaan* you'd think *she* was King of France the way people *persist* in praising her fucking name! Joan did *this*, Joan did *that*, Joan won *another battle*, Joan /

THOMAS. Literally crowned you?

CHARLES. Ooh! Spicy Thomas!

THOMAS. Forgive me, I /

CHARLES. No! Much more body, less head, very good Thomas! Spicy Thomas!

> (**DANCER TWO,** *who* **CHARLES** *is wrapped around, suddenly stops.*)

DANCER TWO. In truth Joan is a mighty soldier.

CHARLES. (*Annoyed.*) Oh is she?

DANCER TWO. I fought with them on the battlefield. Me?! In the mud and the blood and /.. I was terrified at first, of course, terrified! But when I drew near I saw Joan's eyes shone brightly. "*Have no fear,*" they said, "*For you are fuelled by God. You have all the power you need* *inside of you. Let it out! Let it out!"* And their look to me was, *so inspired*, I, their face, *shone*! And I have never felt so strong! Never felt so *sure*! So I raised my sword and I ran and I fought and I roared and I roared and I *roared*! ...That power was *inside me*, the whole time?! Joan showed me how to let it out /

CHARLES. Yes yes! I hear similar stories each and every fucking day! Joan is *amazing*! The *incredible* Joan! Joan Joan *JOAN*! Joan Joan *JOAN*! Joan Joan Joan Joan /

     (**CHARLES** *spins and almost falls.*)

Ohhh!

MAN ONE. Careful, sir!

CHARLES. It's slippy there!

MAN TWO. Yes sir!

THOMAS. Come and sit down /

CHARLES. No no, I'm fine! I'm *fine*!

THOMAS. You're starting to embarrass yourself /

CHARLES. *I'm fine!* ...*You* need to loosen up! It's a *party* for sucksake!

THOMAS. Yes, well, it's been a party for weeks now. How much longer will everyone be here /

CHARLES. They love it!

THOMAS. Yes but, *perhaps* we should be getting back to work? *Perhaps* you should speak with Joan /

CHARLES. *(Taunting.)* Perhaps perhaps perhaps!

THOMAS. Why do you keep me here if you don't listen to me?! You don't respect me /

CHARLES. Oh Thomas! Have a drink!

(**CHARLES** *reaches for another drink.* **THOMAS** *stops him.* **CHARLES** *lets* **THOMAS**'s *hand stay on his.*)

THOMAS. Look. I know this has all been, quite sudden. And it's huge! And you've wanted it, forever! It'd be understandable if you felt, uncertain. But you can do this, I believe in you. Joan does too.

(**CHARLES** *clocks the kindness, then bats it away, and grabs the bottle.*)

CHARLES. Oh have a drink! Have a drink Thomas!

THOMAS. No, no thank you.

CHARLES. Why not?

THOMAS. I'm working, sir.

CHARLES. You know, you've become really rather dull Thomas. Your face. Was once quite pleasant to look at, and yet, in this light? It's honestly quite dull.

THOMAS. .

CHARLES. You're in your head again! I can see you!

THOMAS. .

MAN THREE. Sir?

CHARLES. What?!

MAN THREE. Joan sir, will I let her in?

CHARLES. No /

THOMAS. Yes!

MAN THREE. Sir? Am I to send her away?

CHARLES. Yes /

THOMAS. No!

MAN THREE. Sir?

CHARLES. Must I repeat myself?

MAN THREE. Just, just *once* more sir. Will I /

CHARLES. Oh what's the point in being King if people FUCKING IGNORE YOU?!

> (*His rage is frightening, even to himself. Everyone stares.*)

Oh. Fuck it. Show her in.

> (**MAN THREE** *exits.* **CHARLES** *throws himself back into the throb of bodies.* **MAN ONE** *and* **MAN TWO** *whisper to each other over drinks.* **THOMAS** *watches them.* **JOAN** *enters.* **JOAN** *can't see the King at first, then is disgusted when they do. Some* **DANCERS** *flock to* **JOAN** *instantly and dance around them, which annoys* **CHARLES.** **JOAN** *stands still, focused on* **CHARLES.**)

Oh hey, Joan! Welcome to my party!

JOAN. Finally! I've been trying to get in touch with you! It's urgent!

CHARLES. Yeah, everything's always urgent.

JOAN. I told you we have *one* year! The people are dying /

CHARLES. Oh they always are! Come! Come dance, Dance!

JOAN. Are, are you *drunk*?!

CHARLES. I am the King! I am the *King*!

JOAN. You are the King without the capital. We must attack Paris, immediately! You promised we would!

CHARLES. Yes, yes well I /

JOAN. *Straight* after the coronation!

CHARLES. Yes I know, but /

JOAN. But what?!

CHARLES. I, I've been busy! *Very busy!*

JOAN. So I see.

> *(More of the* **DANCERS** *move over to* **JOAN.**
> **CHARLES** *watches them, jealous.* **JOAN** *stands
> confident in their queerness.)*

CHARLES. You're different! You seem, different?

JOAN. .

CHARLES. Come! Come drink with us!

JOAN. Give me leave to go to Paris.

CHARLES. Excuse me? Are you, are you telling me what
to do?!

JOAN. .

CHARLES. I am your King! You serve me!

JOAN. I serve God, sir, as you yourself do.

CHARLES. Stop. *Stop!* I command you to STOP!

> *(Everyone stops and stares at* **CHARLES.**
> **MARIE** *appears.)*

MARIE. Charles? Darling, what's wrong?

CHARLES. It's Joan! She ignores me, she disobeys me!

JOAN. I do not!

CHARLES. You see! You *see*! It's intolerable! She disrespects
me!

DANCERS. They.

CHARLES. What?

DANCERS. They disrespect you.

> *(***JOAN** *can't help but smile.* **CHARLES** *explodes.)*

CHARLES. In Heaven's Name! I, I /.. I am the KING of FRANCE!

YOLANDE. Yes we know, and yet you insist on shouting about it.

> (**YOLANDE** *appears from nowhere and sweeps across the stage.* **CHARLES** *tries to tidy himself up.* **MAN ONE** *and* **MAN TWO** *instantly move to stand behind* **YOLANDE** *and stare at* **JOAN**.)

CHARLES. Well, well no one listens! No one listens to me!

YOLANDE. Sit down Charles, you're drunk. Joan! How wonderful of you to join us!

> (**YOLANDE** *holds out her hand, and* **JOAN** *kisses it.* **MARIE** *does the same.*)

JOAN. Ma'am. I am in great haste to /

YOLANDE. Oh you always are Joan! And yet this is a party! No politics at a party! Now, we have a gift for you.

> (**YOLANDE** *signals and some* **DANCERS** *appear, holding beautiful gowns. They surround* **JOAN**, *who looks horrified.* **YOLANDE** *and* **MARIE** *are beaming.*)

Don't you just love them?!

MAN ONE. Very good ma'am!

MAN TWO. Wonderful!

MARIE. Custom made! And each with a headdress to cover, *(Signals to* **JOAN***'s hair.)* all this, whilst it's growing out.

YOLANDE. And that's not all! We have also prepared introductions to some young gentlemen!

> (**MARIE** *squeals and claps excitedly.*)

As, of course, you yourself have no connections. We have taken the trouble of arranging it for you.

JOAN. Arranging what?

MARIE. There's a line of suitors, Joan! Waiting to meet with you!

YOLANDE. Hand selected by Marie and I.

MARIE. All noble men, with the means to support you. Some are quite handsome!

YOLANDE. And you know, there are some men who actually love a feisty spirit in a woman.

MARIE. Yes, they might even let you hold a sword once in a while!

>   (**YOLANDE** *laughs,* **MEN ONE** *and* **TWO** *join her.*)

YOLANDE. You're a pretty girl, Joan, underneath it all.

MARIE. Yes, quite pretty.

YOLANDE. We're going to help you become a woman. And learn the art of femininity.

MARIE. It's very exciting!

JOAN. .

YOLANDE. I know this must be overwhelming for you. We are protecting your future! But it's a gift we are *happy* to give. We *enjoy* bestowing you with such kindness. For we have decided that from now on, we want you by our side.

MARIE. Yes! You're one of us now, one of the family.

YOLANDE. Your passion and vigour, when channelled carefully, will be very effective at court.

JOAN. At court?

YOLANDE. Yes, I know it's unusual! But I have decided to find you a position! Your mind, Joan, your fire! I want you with me. A lady of court, and we'll /

JOAN. I'm not a lady!

YOLANDE. Oh we do not discriminate here.

MAN ONE. No ma'am.

YOLANDE. Look, Thomas is low born!

MAN TWO. Yes ma'am.

YOLANDE. And, I believe not married, either? So perhaps there's a possible match?

MARIE. Oh Mother, stop playing Cupid!

YOLANDE. Oh I can't help it! I am a romantic at heart! Now, let's get you changed, and we can begin with lessons in etiquette.

JOAN. No!

MARIE. Joan? What's wrong?!

JOAN. I can't wear that! I can't wear that, I need my armour, I have work to do!

YOLANDE. Oh Joan, always so passionate! Bless you! Look, you've done a marvellous job, truly. And for a young, illiterate, peasant girl, to have achieved what you have? It's incredible!

MARIE. We thank you for your service.

MEN ONE & TWO. Yes.

JOAN. I don't understand?

MARIE. It's over, Joan! You can relax in the satisfaction that you have contributed greatly to the war and /

JOAN. No! No it's not *over*! We are barely beginning! I must return to battle, immediately!

YOLANDE. *(Chuckles.)* Ah yes. I understand the pull, for I myself have frequented the battlefield in my youth. I know the exhilaration, the mud and the blood. Yes! But you'll grow out of it, I promise you. And motherhood is its own kind of adventure.

JOAN. Motherhood? No! I, I will be neither mother nor wife!

(**MARIE** *gasps. Everyone stares at* **JOAN.**)

MARIE. So the rumours are true! You do possess, unnatural desires.

JOAN. The only desire I have is to free France! We must attack Paris! *Immediately!*

MARIE. Young lady?! You forget yourself!

JOAN. You forget the cause! You abandon the people!

YOLANDE. Now listen! I have offered you nothing but my support, from the very beginning. When others had doubts I supported you, unquestionably. I, myself, have financially funded your campaign! But I am not a bottomless pit! When will it end?

JOAN. When we have justice! When we liberate our people!

YOLANDE. Oh dear Joan. I believed in you, I believed your vision to be good. But ambition, it seems, grows like mould in the minds of even the purest of beings.

MARIE. Yes, such a shame!

YOLANDE. And so it behoves me to practise realistic politics. For the good of this country.

MAN ONE. Hear hear.

YOLANDE. There is *no need* to progress to Paris. It is an expensive and dangerous pursuit of personal power that I simply cannot support.

JOAN. Personal power?! This is not about me! I serve God! I am guided to act immediately /

YOLANDE. I seriously question your ability to read such guidance, if this be the delivery of it. Joan you're being so, so abrasive?

MARIE. Yes, it's quite aggressive!

JOAN. Forgive me, my delivery, madam. I am simply passionate about the cause!

MARIE. And we are not?

JOAN. *(Getting frustrated.)* No, no that's not what I /

MARIE. If you are questioning my devotion to this country, then you are seriously misguided!

JOAN. *(Snapping.)* No! No madam, I /

YOLANDE. Gosh! You know, I thought us the same. Passionate women. Powerful women. Women with sense, in this world of ridiculous men!

> *(**MEN ONE** and **TWO** shuffle uncomfortably.)*

But you're not that, you're not, you're not like a woman at all are you? You're, you're /.. Well, I don't quite know what you are?!

> *(**MARIE** sniggers.)*

MARIE. A beast.

> *(Everyone laughs at **JOAN**. **YOLANDE** doesn't laugh but stares. **JOAN** spins, hurt.)*

JOAN. I looked up to you.

YOLANDE. Oh darling, I get it, I really do. For I am well-seasoned in the art of politics. I have fought, for *decades*, to be in the position I am now. Battled my way through this world of tedious men. All their endless arrogance. All their smug superiority. All their unwanted touches and gaze upon my female form. I have suffered, in silence, the injustices put upon my sex. But I have never *once* complained! I never made a fuss, I always maintained my grace. Oh yes, I've sacrificed! I've swallowed back my pride, bit my lip, bided my time. I fought with men, and flattered men, and married men and bore their children. I played them all at their own game and look where I am now! I did *all this*, alone! Did it all so young women like you could have something to aspire to. So you too can imagine standing beside The King. I did this for you. And *look*!

> (**YOLANDE** *spins slowly on the spot, arms outstretched, proud.* **MEN ONE** *and* **TWO** *bow their heads respectfully.* **MARIE** *smiles adoringly at her mother.*)

This is *my house*! I built it. We have The Crown! My daughter is his wife!

JOAN. And you call this victory?

YOLANDE & MARIE. Yes!

JOAN. Oh. Oh I thought you more than this. Thought you wanted more, than this /

YOLANDE. More? *More?!* Are the sacrifices I made not enough? Are the rights I fought for not enough? I *paid*, for *you* to *fight*!

JOAN. I thought we were fighting the same fight!

YOLANDE. And you dare to ask for *more*? You insult me!

MARIE. Yes it's too much! You ask too much, *you're* too much /

JOAN. Maybe, or you're not enough.

> (*Dangerous silence.* **YOLANDE** *seethes.*)

YOLANDE. Out-rageous! Dangerous! Beast! Mannish Brute!

JOAN. I thought you wanted freedom, for France. But really you just want power, this is all about *your* power?

CHARLES. No it's about mine.

> (*Everyone stares at* **CHARLES.** *He clicks, and* **MARIE** *shrinks herself to fit under his arm.*

YOLANDE *walks slowly across the stage to stand behind* CHARLES *and* MARIE. JOAN *watches, horrified.* CHARLES *fiddles with* MARIE'*s hair.*)

This is all getting rather tedious Joan.

JOAN. Yes sir, it is! For still I am denied? The clock is ticking, we must march upon Paris immediately!

CHARLES. Must we?

JOAN. Yes! And then straight onto Rouen, as we have always agreed /

CHARLES. Oh Joan! Can't we just enjoy this? This here, *look*! It's wonderful!

JOAN. No!

(*Everyone is stunned.*)

CHARLES. No?

JOAN. Forgive me sir, it's just it's, it's *not about us*! It's about the People! A great change is happening! The people are thinking new thoughts, they're stepping into a new way of being. Fighting for freedom, to live as they live, and love as they love. *You* have inspired that! It's People-powered, this movement, this great Revolution!

YOLANDE. Who gave you authority to start a *Revolution*?

(*Silence. Everyone stares at* JOAN.)

JOAN. Sir, sir please, I /

CHARLES. D'you know never *once* am I visited by God! Never once hast there been explicit guidance for *me*?! No blinding light! No holy message! No Divine communion *for me*?!

MARIE. Charles, sit down darling, we'll order you some /

CHARLES. No no no the King of France! I am the *King*! Why does God not send his messages to me?!

MARIE. Heaven only knows /

CHARLES. And yet *she* is the chosen one? Why is that?! *Why* is that?!

MAN ONE. Sir, we could have her arrested.

CHARLES. *(Confused.)* Arrested?

MAN TWO. Yes! Before she causes a mutiny!

THOMAS. Mutiny? Joan?! She's the purest being I know!

(**CHARLES** *spins, drunk and confused.*)

MAN THREE. Yes, come gentlemen! What is this?

MAN TWO. She's growing too ambitious!

MAN ONE. It's too great a risk!

MAN THREE. Her motives are pure!

MAN ONE. We are beginning to doubt that.

MAN THREE. Well this is the first I've heard of such doubts. Are we not a court of men who /

MAN TWO. You've been busy!

MAN THREE. Babysitting Charles, at *your* request! Whilst you've been discussing matters without my involvement?

MAN ONE. Not everything requires your involvement. You are a *junior* member of court /

MAN THREE. My voice deserves to be heard!

THOMAS. As does mine! Sir?

YOLANDE. Charles! Let me take care of this. We are, as you know, beginning negotiations with the English /

CHARLES. What? What negotiations?

YOLANDE. Merely speculative, of course, until your approval.

MAN THREE. What negotiations?

THOMAS. Why wasn't I informed?

MARIE. Who are *you* to be informed? *(To **CHARLES**.)* Darling, we are discussing a treaty /

THOMAS, JOAN & MAN THREE. What?!

YOLANDE. We are on the *cusp* of an arrangement /

JOAN. No /

YOLANDE. To bring *peace* to this land!

JOAN. Oh come now!

YOLANDE. Excuse me?!

JOAN. We all know peace may be had *only* at the point of the sword /

YOLANDE. At the point of the pen /

CHARLES. At the point of the King's tongue! For it is I who shall decide the course of action! Neither the negotiator nor the warrior, but the King! I am the King! *I* am the King! I AM THE *FUCKING KING*!

ALL. Sir.

YOLANDE. Charles, we merely *began* to make arrangements /

CHARLES. Without my consent?

MARIE. Oh, we didn't want to bother you with it darling!

CHARLES. Bother me? *Bother*, me. Didn't want, to, *bother*, right you can go to Paris.

(Silence. Everyone is stunned.)

YOLANDE. Charles!

CHARLES. I am the King, I decide.

(Everyone is still stunned.)

CHARLES. *(To* JOAN.*)* Off you go.

JOAN. *(Exploding into action.)* Thank you sir, thank you!
I won't let you down!

> (JOAN *rushes off upstage, taking most of
> the* DANCERS *with them.* CHARLES *pulls one
> of the* DANCERS *back from* JOAN's *mob as
> they pass. He wraps the* DANCER *around
> him, eyeballing* MARIE. MARIE *marches off,
> in tears.* YOLANDE *glares at* CHARLES, *then
> follows* MARIE. *Upstage, with their backs to
> us,* JOAN *and the* DANCERS' *bodies shudder
> and shake, preparing for war. Downstage,*
> CHARLES *winds with his* DANCER, *watching*
> THOMAS, *who's stuck, unsure.* THOMAS
> *decides to follow* JOAN.*)*

CHARLES. Thomas?

> (THOMAS *stops.)*

Sweet little Thomas. Be careful now.

Scene Two

> (**THOMAS** *is sucked into the throb of bodies upstage.* **JOAN** *turns and leads their* **ARMY** *downstage. They gather momentum, fierce and powerful like before.* **JOAN** *is in their element, full of swagger.* **JOAN'S ARMY** *chants* **JOAN***'s name. It builds and builds and builds. Then, suddenly, they are stuck. Their bodies jam, refusing to let them move.* **JOAN** *cries out in frustration. The* **ARMY***'s formation breaks, and they catch their breath, bent double and confused at their own bodies.*)

JOAN. Why do you stop? Why do you stop?!

> (**JOAN** *spins, panicked. They turn to us.*)

They ignore me! Yolande has got to them? They think me wild, think me mad?

> (**JOAN** *spins, spots* **THOMAS.***)

Thomas! Why do we stop?

THOMAS. We have not received word from the King.

JOAN. What?! Where is he?!

THOMAS. I know not!

JOAN. He promised to fight with us! Where is he? WHERE IS HE?

THOMAS. Joan?! Don't shout at me!

> (*Everyone stares at* **JOAN** *and* **THOMAS.***)

JOAN. I'm sorry, I /.. I'm sorry.

THOMAS. I'll ask the men.

> (**THOMAS** *exits.* **JOAN** *spins, feeling everyone staring.*)

JOAN. *(To us.)* They stare at me, they're staring?! Think me ugly? They think me mannish, some "mannish brute"?!

(JOAN *spins, spots* DUNOIS.)

Dunois!

DUNOIS. Here we are again! They just can't keep us away eh?

JOAN. Where is the King?

DUNOIS. *(Shrugs.)* I wouldn't dare presume to know.

JOAN. He promised to follow us here to Paris! He *promised* more soldiers, he promised to fight with us!

DUNOIS. He has promised many things many times.

JOAN. What do you mean?!

DUNOIS. Welcome to politics Joan.

(THOMAS *appears.*)

JOAN. News?!

THOMAS. Nothing. No sign of the King.

JOAN. Where is he?! Why this strange absence?

DUNOIS. I don't know, but we can do nothing without his consent. We must sit tight and wait for news. But I must be honest, I fear our position *here* is vulnerable.

JOAN. Nonsense. We are strong! I am strong!

DUNOIS. I'm not doubting your strength Joan, I'm merely stating a fact about our location. We can't stay here.

JOAN. So we cannot proceed and we cannot stay here? You can't be suggesting a retreat! We can win this! We can take Paris!

DUNOIS. The English are strong in their defence, organised and well equipped. For they've had much time to prepare. Our delay may indeed be our downfall.

JOAN. I *tried* to convince the King. For *weeks* I tried! And still he /

DUNOIS. I know, I know! We're on your side, remember.

THOMAS. Joan, are you all right?

JOAN. I'm fine! I'm fine!

DUNOIS. Meanwhile the Parisians are proving less than friendly.

JOAN. What? Why? We are here to liberate them!

DUNOIS. Well they don't seem to want liberation, kid. Some are even fighting back.

JOAN. What?!

DUNOIS. I don't understand it either. Every other city has opened the gates for us happily, gratefully! Something isn't right! It's not like before, where we had the wind at our backs. Something isn't right, the, the timing perhaps? The fates, as you'd say, don't seem to be aligned.

JOAN. Dunois! *Never* have I seen you doubt our cause?!

DUNOIS. Never have I doubted, and I doubt you not now. I am completely committed to you kid. I mean, I've *never* felt God so clearly as when I'm with you. I'll follow you anywhere. But I cannot deny my own instincts. Everything is telling me no, and I have to protect these men.

JOAN. They will be safe! For we are fuelled by God!

DUNOIS. We know God is with you Joan, but we men are earthbound. We simply cannot win Paris under these circumstances, it's impossible.

JOAN. Nothing is impossible! We have proved that again and again! We must attack!

THOMAS. We cannot attempt an attack in the absence of the King for whom we are fighting!

JOAN. Why not?

THOMAS. It's the system!

JOAN. Fuck the system!

DUNOIS. Woah, careful kid, that's anarchy.

THOMAS. *Think* Joan, think it through! Without the King we have nothing. We either all die, or we somehow miraculously take Paris, and then what? Are *you* going to be King? We must wait until we /

JOAN. You always want to wait! At Orléans you were the same /

THOMAS. And you ignored me /

JOAN. And look how that worked out! Beautifully! Because the People rose to fight with me!

THOMAS. But the people *here* are not joining you!

JOAN. They will! Our delay is our downfall, Dunois is right /

DUNOIS. Thank you /

JOAN. It's taken us *so* long to get here, they have given up hope! So now we have to fight through their fear *and* the English! And the longer we wait the worse it will be. They have forgotten who I am! The people of Paris will never be free!

THOMAS. They don't *want* to be free! They stand against us!

JOAN. They are against us now because they do not know I can liberate their thinking! If I can just get to them, speak to them, I can show them a new way!

THOMAS. I fear you are misguided! Exhausted, perhaps?! Joan, are you unwell?

JOAN. I'm fine!

THOMAS. Yet unable to see what is so clearly true?

JOAN. Oh will you forever be so cowardly Thomas?

THOMAS. I am no coward! I'll fight by your side to the very end! But I will not stand by and let you make such wild decisions, simply to save face!

JOAN. Is that what you think I'm doing?!

THOMAS. I see no other reason!

JOAN. Freedom! I promised them freedom! And we are *so close*! Perhaps you can wait but I cannot! The people I fight for are dying!

THOMAS. More will die today if you push forward foolishly!

DUNOIS. He's right. Don't let us die for nothing. You'll be remembered Joan, we won't. And look I'd happily die to support your name, we all would, but let's make it count eh? Let's make it count! An attack on Paris now, without the King, is not going to count in the way we need it to.

(**SOLDIER ONE** *bursts in.*)

SOLDIER ONE. News from the King!

JOAN. Yes?

THOMAS. He has come, with soldiers and supplies, as he promised /

SOLDIER ONE. No! He has abandoned the route to Paris!

(**JOAN** *is suddenly dead still.*)

JOAN. Abandoned?

SOLDIER ONE. The King and his army have turned south, toward the Loire.

JOAN. Abandoned?! No, no he wouldn't!

DUNOIS. He has. Selfish bastard!

JOAN. Treason! If you speak ill of him!

DUNOIS. His actions speak loud enough!

THOMAS. What will we do?

DUNOIS. We must retreat.

THOMAS. Oh thank God!

JOAN. No!

DUNOIS. Joan, we must! We have no choice! *(To* **SOLDIER ONE.***)* Sound the retreat!

JOAN. No! Wait! Wait! I order you to wait!

DUNOIS. Joan?

JOAN. Just, wait, one moment, please!

> *(***JOAN** *spins, completely frazzled. They turn to us.)*

Oh God! What is happening?! I have always done everything you asked me. I've served Charles humbly. Why does he abandon me now?! How could he do such a thing?! Charles was chosen by *you* God to be King, and he /.. He, he *was* chosen?! ...Charles was chosen to be King, by Divine right, by Holy order? Yes, yes he must have been or else, or else he's, just a man? /.. Just a man?! /.. I have been serving a man? A simple, man. Oh God! I have got so caught up in the system I, I forgot the power you gave me?! Please, please God direct my thinking, for I *think* I am being asked to transcend even my own thoughts? I must go beyond even my wildest imagination? I must serve God, without the King?!

DUNOIS. Joan? What are your orders?

> *(Everyone stares at* **JOAN.***)*

JOAN. *(To us.)* They are waiting for my command. *My* command?

THOMAS. Joan? We need to move!

JOAN. *(To us.)* What am I to do, surrender to the King? Or fight alone for God?

DUNOIS. Joan?!

JOAN. Fight! We fight on! We attack Paris!

THOMAS. What?! Joan no! To disobey the King is treason!

JOAN. The King has abandoned us! But I shall not abandon thee. I will *never* surrender! *(To* **DUNOIS.***)* I will *never* retreat!

DUNOIS. If you're sure?

THOMAS. Dunois! No!

SOLDIER ONE. Sir?

JOAN. If he does not enter Paris as King, then I will as Joan. We attack, now! We ATTACK!

> *(Battle drums, hard and loud.* **JOAN** *bursts into war-dance.* **JOAN'S ARMY** *joins them.)*

WE ARE THE MIGHTY! WE ARE GOD'S WARRIORS!

> *(***JOAN'S ARMY** *cheers.)*

I WILL LEAD YOU TO VICTORY! TO FREEDOM! I AM FUELLED BY GOD! I AM JOAN!

> *(***JOAN'S ARMY** *cheers.)*

I AM JOAN! I AM JOAN!

> *(Like an arrogant rockstar,* **JOAN** *struts up and down.* **JOAN** *dances, full of swagger and sex.* **JOAN'S ARMY** *cheers and chants* **JOAN***'s name. An English archer suddenly sends an arrow through* **JOAN***'s leg.* **JOAN** *cries out in pain and falls.* **JOAN'S ARMY** *panics. Blood pumps everywhere.)*

THOMAS. Oh God!

JOAN. Onwards! Onwards!

THOMAS. You must lie still! You must lie *still*!

JOAN. Onwards!

THOMAS. We must retreat?!

DUNOIS. Yes!

JOAN. No! Never!

DUNOIS. We must!

JOAN. Never! I am Joan! I am *Joan*!

> (**JOAN** *pulls themself up and, with the arrow still in their leg, begins the war-dance.* **JOAN'S ARMY** *stares, amazed.* **JOAN** *is trying their best but is betrayed by their body. It's heartbreaking.*)

THOMAS. Oh stop! Please!

DUNOIS. I'm calling the retreat!

JOAN. No!

THOMAS. You are injured and we are outnumbered! Anything but retreat is absurd!

JOAN. No! No! We must fight on!

THOMAS. Joan, it's *over*!

JOAN. No! I will not stop! I will *never* stop!

DUNOIS. Hey kid, it's okay it's okay! You did really well /

JOAN. No! No!

DUNOIS. Take her to safety! Lift her!

JOAN. NO!

(**JOAN** *loses all control, a wild animal.* **JOAN**
*is dragged, kicking and screaming from the
battlefield.* **JOAN** *is lifted high into the air.
The arrow is removed from* **JOAN***'s thigh and
they cry out, then faint.* **JOAN** *is carried to
centre stage, where a bed appears. They are
stripped of their armour and laid upon the
bed. The battle drums die away.* **JOAN** *is left
alone.)*

Scene Three

> (**JOAN** *wakes and stares at the walls, depressed.*
> **JOAN** *lifts one hand and looks at it, wiggles*
> *their fingers a little, catches sight of us.*)

JOAN. I was on fire once. My insides alight, divinely inspired, my body burned bright, lit up the whole sky with white hot fury and fire! ...As a child, I knew. I was *full*, of unused fuel. Stuck in my blood. Trapped, under this skin. Latent potential sat patient in my bones, biding its time, waiting for a spark, God lit the match and boom! And oh! How we blazed! ...Now? I am ash. Black crispy cinders. Soot.

> (**JOAN** *lifts both hands and speaks to them.*)

Still here? For what purpose?

> (**JOAN** *shows us their hands, and waits.*)

I see none.

> (**DANCER ONE** *enters with a dress.*)

No. Take it away!

DANCER ONE. Will you not get dressed again today?

JOAN. I said no!

DANCER ONE. I'll leave it here for you, in case you change your /

JOAN. Dare you question me?! Don't you know who I am?! I am Joan! *I am Joan!*

> (**JOAN** *throws the dress at the* **DANCER,** *then instantly regrets it.*)

Oh I'm sorry! I /..

(They catch sight of us and are disgusted with themself.)

(To us.) Oh God, what have I become? Who is this? I don't recognise myself I /.. Will I always feel this heavy?

(JOAN picks up the dress and tries to rip it in two. DANCER ONE stares. JOAN opens a wooden chest of clothes. They urgently try everything on, unsatisfied with anything. Dysphoria in their body. Teenage angst. They cry out. Then hit the side of their own head repeatedly.)

Stupid stupid stupid stupid stupid!

DANCER ONE. Stop that!

JOAN. Go away!

DANCER ONE. Ma'am please!

JOAN. Call me that again and you'll know of it!

DANCER ONE. Yes, forgive me, I /

JOAN. Get out!

(DANCER ONE looks at JOAN, maternal and knowing. JOAN can't bear it.)

What?!

DANCER ONE. I know the emptiness you're feeling.

JOAN. I doubt it!

DANCER ONE. I know it burns deep inside you. Burns a hole so deep, and so dark, like it's hollowed you out.

JOAN. .

DANCER ONE. But you won't feel like this forever, I promise you. Something or someone will come along, completely unexpected, and inspire you. You were that for me, when I needed it most! Keep the faith Joan, this too shall pass /

JOAN. You know nothing! Nothing! Nobody knows!

DANCER ONE. Very well. Thomas is outside /

JOAN. No!

DANCER ONE. I told him you wouldn't see him, and yet he refuses to leave /

JOAN. Then tell him again!

DANCER ONE. He's been waiting for days. He insists he must see you. He's a good friend /

JOAN. No /

DANCER ONE. You need to see your friends. I'm letting him in.

JOAN. No, no! You cannot! You cannot disobey me!

> (**DANCER ONE** *exits, and* **THOMAS** *enters.*
> **JOAN** *tries to be angry, but hugs him instead.*)

THOMAS. Joan! Oh Joan! I've been waiting outside your door, day and night, so worried about you! They wouldn't let me in?!

JOAN. I couldn't see you. I was so ashamed!

THOMAS. Why?!

JOAN. Oh Thomas, I *lost*! I lost and now *I* am lost!

THOMAS. No!

JOAN. For what purpose do I have now? What reason do I have for being?

THOMAS. Come on Joan, pick yourself up! Every great warrior suffers defeat! You lost one battle, but we can still win the war. We can, and we *must*!

JOAN. How?! When my heart is so broken?! How could he betray us so coldly?

THOMAS. We don't know all the details, we mustn't assume /

JOAN. What's happening at court?

THOMAS. I don't know, I don't know, I've been here. Charles ordered me to stay here, to take care of you.

JOAN. I bet they're writing up the Treaty right now, without us!

THOMAS. No, Charles wouldn't do that, he respects you too much! He sent me here to protect you /

JOAN. He abandoned me! He hates me!

THOMAS. He *loves* you! He will call for you soon, I'm sure of it. He will call for you to fight again, and fight you will, and victoriously! So we must be patient and prepare /

JOAN. No no no you don't understand, he *hates* me /

THOMAS. No /

JOAN. I know it! Yolande has got in his ear because *she* hates me, and now *he* does too, they *all* do!

THOMAS. Come now! Come! Keep the faith /

JOAN. Do you hate me?

THOMAS. What?! Of course not! How could I hate you?

JOAN. I don't know! I /.. It's broken, something is broken Thomas, I can feel it!

THOMAS. Nonsense! Nothing is broken. I love you, the King loves you, everything is well. You've just lost your confidence is all. You'll be back on your feet, fighting for France in no time at all! And I by your side, as always /

JOAN. What France will I be fighting for?

THOMAS. What?

JOAN. What is the strategy now?

THOMAS. I, I don't know.

JOAN. No, nobody does.

THOMAS. But look, one thing at a time. First, you need to rest, cus you're exhausted! You need to get better then we can move forward /

JOAN. Move forward how? Move forward where? What does that actually mean?

THOMAS. He will call for you soon. Call for you to fight /

JOAN. They drag me from battle! They don't want me to fight, they want me constrained! Trapped in the chains that have held France back for generations!

THOMAS. No, no that's not true!

JOAN. What are they doing *right* now? Laughing at me? Plotting and scheming?

THOMAS. No, no of course not /

JOAN. What does he want with me now? To swan around court in a corset? I am a warrior! I'm not one of them!

THOMAS. But you could be! You could *learn* to be at court. And be *brilliant* at it! Be of great service to this country /

JOAN. No /

THOMAS. I'm sure you could, I'm sure I'm sure there is a way forward /

JOAN. No! Can't you see I can't pretend to be someone I'm not?! I *have* to be myself! I have no choice! I can't bend out of shape like you do, trying my best to fit in, lying to myself and jumping whenever Charles calls?!

THOMAS. You may mock me, but I /

JOAN. That's not what I /

THOMAS. I've done what I needed to in order to survive. I won't be shamed for that!

JOAN. Thomas, I'm sorry /

THOMAS. And I'm proud of the work I have done! For this country, I have achieved great things. I've been living as an outsider in this court for longer than you can imagine. Do not speak to me of fitting in. I've worked my way up from *nothing*! I've learnt how to play their game /

JOAN. We don't need to /

THOMAS. You play their game, *then* you get powerful enough to change it from the inside. You manage upwards.

JOAN. Charles won't change!

THOMAS. He will, he will. I *know* him. I know he can change.

JOAN. And what if he can't? What if his fear is so great it swallows him whole? Taking this country and its people down with him?

THOMAS. We must be patient! And trust in the good works these men are doing! The King and his council are negotiating a treaty with the English /

JOAN. No /

THOMAS. And we should at least consider their attempts at peace! For they are seasoned with experience far greater than ours!

JOAN. Peace?!

THOMAS. Yes! Are we not fighting for peace?

JOAN. No! Justice! We are fighting for justice /

THOMAS. One and the same!

JOAN. No! No not at all the same! I will not *compromise* my country, I will not *betray* my people!

THOMAS. *Your* people?

JOAN. They invade our homes, burn our villages, kill our people. And you want to arrange *peace*? Cutting up this land of ours on your maps, and your charts /

THOMAS. So when will it end? When will it end?! As brilliant as you are Joan, *when* will you stop /

JOAN. When we have Justice! When we have Revolution! I am called to lead the charge, *I* am chosen!

THOMAS. And I am not! Not all of us can afford the luxury of *revolution*. I do not have the wind at my back like you Joan, I don't have a God to believe in like you!

JOAN. Jealousy? Is this, jealousy?

THOMAS. No it's the truth! I love you, and I fear you've gone too far.

JOAN. Oh! Oh Thomas, you too? They have wormed their way inside your sweet sweet heart too?

THOMAS. No /

JOAN. I thought you were different, but you're just the same! Just the same as *all those men* at court /

THOMAS. Don't be foolish! I am so clearly on your side! I'm simply suggesting you slow down enough to *think*!

JOAN. How much did they pay you?

THOMAS. .

JOAN. How much?

THOMAS. How dare you? I have always, and will forever be, your greatest champion.

JOAN. And yet you betray me now?

THOMAS. The betrayal is all yours if you describe me thus.

JOAN. Get out. Get out! I never want to see your lying face again. You're a liar! You're a coward! A dirty traitor! Judas! Get out! GET OUT!

THOMAS. I thought us friends. My mistake.

> (**THOMAS** *leaves.* **JOAN** *paces, high on adrenaline, then suddenly regrets it.*)

JOAN. Thomas?! Thomas!

> *(He doesn't return.* **JOAN** *beats themself up.)*

Argh!

> *(Five* **AFAB DANCERS** *enter and stand in a clump centre stage, like some weird Greek chorus.* **JOAN** *looks at them, unsure.)*

Hello?

DANCER ONE. We have an urgent message /

ALL DANCERS. From the King!

JOAN. I thought you worked for me, fought with me?

> *(The* **DANCERS** *shift, embarrassed, but stand firm.)*

DANCER ONE. We have, an urgent message /

ALL DANCERS. From the King!

JOAN. Very well. What is it?

DANCER TWO. He did not wish to be apart from you for so long, his /

ALL DANCERS. Bravest soldier.

DANCER ONE. He understands how devastating the loss at Paris will have been for you.

DANCER TWO. And so to offer you a chance to /

ALL DANCERS. Regain your confidence /

DANCER TWO. And to /

ALL DANCERS. Serve the country /

DANCER TWO. You so love, it is required that you /

ALL DANCERS. Raise the siege at Compiegne.

DANCER TWO. And liberate the people there. You are to leave /

JOAN. Compiegne?

DANCER ONE. Yes.

DANCER TWO. You are to leave immediately /

DANCER ONE. Following the route suggested by /

JOAN. Compiegne? Is he in jest?

> (*The* **DANCERS** *shake their heads, their faces blank.*)

Why there?! It makes no sense.

DANCER ONE. The people there are desperate for your aid.

DANCER TWO. They eagerly await your arrival.

JOAN. Compiegne? No, no this, doesn't feel right? And why are you behaving so strangely?

> (*The* **DANCERS**' *faces are blank.*)

I /..

> (**JOAN** *spins, turns to us.*)

Something, here, deep in my belly, a warning? He's laughing at me? I'm being laughed at? Sent away to get rid of me, or sent straight to danger, no no of course not! He wouldn't do that, to even think so would be treason! But still this, warning, feeling, this sense of, something isn't right. My body is trying to tell me /

DANCER THREE. Madam?

> (**JOAN** *freezes, their body jolted.*)

DANCER FOUR. Madam?

> (**JOAN**'s *body jolts again.*)

DANCER FIVE. Madam are you well?

JOAN. Don't! Please!

DANCER FOUR. Don't what?

JOAN. That word, you *know* that word is /.. Please don't call me that!

DANCER THREE. Call you what, madam?

(**JOAN***'s body jolts.*)

JOAN. That word it's /.. Not the right word for me, I! /..

DANCER THREE. Oh! Forgive us, please!

DANCER FOUR. To what should we refer you then?

DANCER FIVE. Sir?

(*The* **DANCERS** *stare, expressionless.* **JOAN** *thrashes and squirms in shame, pulling at their skin.* **DANCERS ONE** *and* **TWO** *look across at the other* **DANCERS***, checking their faces, finding them blank.* **DANCER TWO** *can't bear it anymore.*)

DANCER TWO. Joan!

(**JOAN** *suddenly stops and stands still, tired.*)

What shall we tell the King?

JOAN. *(Quietly.)* I don't know, I, I /..

DANCER ONE. Joan, I'm sorry, but we need a decision, quickly!

JOAN. I, I, well did he say any more? Of the purpose? Or the means? Or whom it is will accompany me?

(*All the* **DANCERS** *shake their heads.*)

That's very odd. Isn't that odd?

(*The* **DANCERS** *stare, expressionless.*)

JOAN. Well, I shall select my own army. Dunois, of course, and Thomas too /

DANCER THREE. They're both away.

JOAN. Away?!

DANCER FOUR. Called on urgent business, this morning.

JOAN. .

DANCER FIVE. But there are *many* other soldiers you could take with you /

DANCER FOUR. Many! And *all* would serve you gladly!

JOAN. .

DANCER ONE. Joan?

JOAN. Something feels odd!

DANCER THREE. We are pressed for time madam.

　　　　(**JOAN***'s body jolts.*)

DANCER FOUR. We need a decision.

DANCER FIVE. They're outside! They're waiting!

DANCER THREE. What will we tell them?

JOAN. I, I /..

　　　　(**JOAN** *spins, panicked, tries to pray to us.*)

Oh God, what do I do? I felt a warning here, something somewhere in my body, about to tell me something. But then that *word*, they keep calling me that word, do they not realise?! /.. I am jolted, every time, my body is /.. Where is my body? I can't feel /.. God I can't hear you, my ears are full of shame I can't hear you, I can't hear /

DANCER TWO. Joan?

JOAN. *(To us.)* I can't hear you God!

DANCER ONE. Have you instruction?

JOAN. *(To us.)* I can't hear I can't /

DANCER FIVE. We must return to the King!

DANCER TWO. Joan?

DANCER THREE. We will report that you /

JOAN. *(To the* **DANCERS.***)* No! No I, yes, yes I will do as the King requests.

Scene Four

> *(The* **DANCERS** *help* **JOAN** *pull on their armour.* **JOAN** *looks vacant, zapped of energy. They begin the war-dance, with many fewer* **SOLDIERS** *and much less energy than before.* **JOAN'S ARMY** *seems tired, less passionate.* **JOAN** *has less power, less command of their own* **ARMY**. *We really feel the absence of* **THOMAS** *and* **DUNOIS**. *One* **DANCER** *suddenly stops.)*

SOLDIER TWO. Please! We are exhausted!

SOLDIER ONE. Yes! As you yourself must also be!

JOAN. No! I am on my feet still!

DANCER TWO. You haven't slept in *days*!

DANCER ONE. Please! We must *rest*!

JOAN. No! No rest! This town is desperately waiting for our arrival! We are going to liberate them. Come, come, put your whole soul into the charge! Onwards!

> *(***JOAN** *begins the war-dance again and their* **ARMY** *reluctantly joins in.* **JOAN** *struggles to command them. One* **SOLDIER** *suddenly stops.)*

SOLDIER THREE. They won't grant us entry!

JOAN. What?

SOLDIER THREE. The people of Compiegne, they won't let us through!

JOAN. They must!

DANCER ONE. They refuse!

JOAN. But Charles said they were waiting for us?! He said they were *desperate* for us to come help them?!

SOLDIER TWO. They won't let us through!

DANCER TWO. What should we do?

SOLDIER ONE. We must retreat!

JOAN. Never!

SOLDIER TWO. Dunois would order retreat!

DANCER TWO. Well he ain't here!

SOLDIER ONE. We need to move. We're not safe here!

JOAN. We're not safe we're not safe we're not safe!

DANCER TWO. *(Alarmed.)* Joan?!

JOAN. *You're* not safe!

DANCER TWO. What?!

JOAN. Nothing! *(To us.)* Who can I trust? How will I know?

SOLDIER THREE. News from the people of Compiegne!

JOAN. Yes?

SOLDIER THREE. They pledge allegiance to the English!

DANCER TWO. What?!

DANCER ONE. They were supposed to be on our side?!

JOAN. You see?! They don't want me! They don't want me it's broken, everything is broken!

SOLDIER THREE. Joan? What are your orders?

JOAN. I /.. I /..

(**JOAN** *panics, tries to pray, can't hear God.*)

SOLDIER THREE. What are your orders?!

DANCER TWO. Joan?

JOAN. .

DANCER ONE. We could head to Margny?

JOAN. What?

DANCER ONE. It's rumoured the defenders of Compiegne have launched an assault /

SOLDIER TWO. Yes! Attacking an outpost!

SOLDIER ONE. Let's go there!

JOAN. No wait! I need to pray!

SOLDIER ONE. We don't have time for *prayer*!

JOAN. I must!

DANCER TWO. Joan?

SOLDIER THREE. Quickly! We have no time!

DANCER TWO. Joan?!

JOAN. Do it!

> (*War-dance with renewed energy. But then the ground they dance on suddenly starts shrinking. They have less space to move, squashed up together, and starting to panic.*)

SOLDIER THREE. We are outnumbered!

SOLDIER TWO. Where are the soldiers we were promised?!

DANCER ONE. They never arrived!

SOLDIER TWO. We must retreat!

JOAN. No! Never! *Never!* We will stand and fight! We will stand and fight to the death!

SOLDIER TWO. Fuck that!

DANCER ONE. She's mad!

SOLDIER THREE. Let's retreat to the town! Quickly!

JOAN. No!

SOLDIER TWO. Yes! Quickly!

JOAN. No! No retreat! No stop! Stop! You cowards! Traitors!
Stay! Stay and fight with me!

> *(The majority of* **JOAN'S ARMY** *leaves.* **JOAN**
> *is left with a handful of frightened* **SOLDIERS**
> *who stare at them desperately.)*

Onwards!

> *(War-dance. Feeble in comparison to usual.*
> *Suddenly, everyone shifts their focus to the*
> *left.* **JOAN** *is a beat behind.)*

SOLDIER ONE. The drawbridge is up!

DANCER TWO. Quickly! To the tower!

JOAN. No wait!

SOLDIER ONE. Quickly! Or we'll be caught!

> *(The* **SOLDIERS** *move to the drawbridge and*
> *squeeze their way through.* **JOAN** *is late to*
> *move and so doesn't keep up. The drawbridge*
> *slams down between* **JOAN** *and the* **SOLDIERS.**
> *Time warps as* **JOAN** *is desperately trapped on*
> *the wrong side of the gate.* **JOAN'S SOLDIERS**
> *helplessly stretch their arms through to*
> **JOAN.** *The* **ENGLISH SOLDIERS** *arrive behind*
> **JOAN. JOAN** *tips their head back and arms*
> *outreached, surrenders to the heavens.)*

JOAN. Dieu m'aide!

> *(***JOAN** *is surrounded by the* **ENGLISH.** *There*
> *is no escape.)*

ENGLISH SOLDIER. Throw down your sword!

JOAN. Jamais!

ENGLISH SOLDIER. Witch!

ENGLISH SOLDIER. We've got her!

ENGLISH SOLDIER. We've got the filthy witch!

ENGLISH SOLDIER. Throw down your sword!

JOAN. *Jamais!*

> *(The* **SOLDIERS** *move tighter around* **JOAN**.
> **JOAN** *tries not to panic, their sword trembling
> in their hand.* **CHARLES** *appears on the
> periphery and watches* **JOAN**. **JOAN** *looks at
> him, then drops their sword. The* **MEN** *grab
> **JOAN** and roughly bundle them. A scrum of
> angry bodies. The* **SOLDIERS** *pick at* **JOAN**'s
> *body over and over.* **JOAN** *tries to escape
> but is pushed down again and again. It's a
> horrible dance, sexually violent, repetitive,
> looping.* **THOMAS** *bursts in and sees the
> scrum of bodies on* **JOAN**.)*

THOMAS. Joan!

> *(***CHARLES** *puts up his hand, and* **THOMAS**'*feet
> are suddenly stuck to the floor. He can't move,
> desperate to help* **JOAN** *or attack* **CHARLES**.)*

You bastard! You *bastard*!

CHARLES. Ah Thomas, how nice of you to /

THOMAS. What the fuck Charles?! *What the fuck?!* You
asked me to look after her? You *used me*?! After
everything we've been through? I *trusted* you!

CHARLES. As well you should, for I am very trustworthy /

THOMAS. Oh God, I told *her* to trust you! She knew
something was wrong, she sensed it! And I pushed her
to trust you?! Oh God this is all my fault!

CHARLES. Sweet little Thomas, stuck in your head again?

THOMAS. She got you the crown! She formed you an army!
What have *you* done? What have you *ever* fucking
done?

CHARLES. Careful now, you're starting to be rude /

THOMAS. What will you do now, eh? What will you do without Joan?

YOLANDE. Rule France.

(**YOLANDE** *appears from nowhere.*)

THOMAS. You betrayed her! Why?! (*To* **CHARLES**.) How could you do this?!

CHARLES. It's not personal Thomas, it's politics.

(**JOAN** *moans in pain.* **CHARLES** *covers his ears.* **YOLANDE** *claps, and the scrum stops moving. The scrum of* **SOLDIERS** *looks at* **YOLANDE**, *waiting for instruction.*)

YOLANDE. Well said Charles. We must always keep in mind the Greater vision we are serving. For France, for the good people of France /

THOMAS. Joan serves the people!

YOLANDE. No, we do. Joan worked for us and she /

THOMAS. She'll be killed! Don't you care?

YOLANDE. (*Genuine.*) Of course I do! I've always liked Joan. I had high hopes for her, and honestly, the disappointment has been most upsetting. Such a waste of talent! That power she has, it's incredible! But far too dangerous when it's not in our hands.

THOMAS. She's innocent! The closest thing to heaven that *you'll* ever see.

CHARLES. Careful Thomas.

YOLANDE. We gave her the chance to prove herself, twice. She failed at Paris and then she failed again at Compiegne. The inconsistency just won't do, especially when the consequences are so catastrophic! Her behaviour at Paris was *reckless*! No, she's becoming an enemy to France. She leaves us no choice!

THOMAS. So you'll just have her killed? Just like that?

YOLANDE. This is war Thomas. You are either with us or you're against us. So, what are *you* going to do?

THOMAS. *(To* **CHARLES.***)* You're better than this! You're a good man, I know you are! Prove it now and save her, save Joan!

CHARLES. *(Quietly.)* I can't.

> *(***THOMAS*** dares to hold* **CHARLES.** **YOLANDE** *is disgusted.)*

THOMAS. You can! Please Charles please!

CHARLES. *(Getting upset.)* Oh don't! This is all very upsetting, *you've* been *very* upsetting, Thomas. *(Holding him.)* Sweet little Thomas!

YOLANDE. *(Interrupting them.)* Yes well, we must of course be professional about all this!

> *(***CHARLES*** pushes* **THOMAS** *away.)*

We must focus our attention on maintaining principles.

THOMAS. Principles?

YOLANDE. Yes. You know yourself, more than most Thomas, the need to compromise. Joan is a necessary sacrifice for the greater good.

THOMAS. How many more centuries will women stand *next* to powerful men? Brilliant women, stuck in a system that won't ever serve them. Won't ever allow them to truly make change. So stuck you turn on other women? Brilliant women, forgotten forever? The only reason Joan will be remembered is because she'll be killed. They'll make a martyr of her, paint her in their image /

CHARLES. She'd be so lucky!

THOMAS. I was a fool to ever think I could change you. Frightened little boy.

CHARLES. I am the King! I am the *King*! Chosen by *God*!

THOMAS. Nah, you're not a King. You're nothing but a bit part in Joan's story. No one will ever remember you for anything good. *(To* **YOLANDE.***)* People will have to search through the history books to even find *your* name! Cus you never dared to change a thing, did you? *(To them both.)* This was never about you. It was always, all about Joan.

YOLANDE. And what about you? A peasant boy who fucked his way up through the ranks? Think anyone will ever remember you?

THOMAS. I doubt it. But that's okay. I'll be rewarded elsewhere.

> *(***THOMAS** *takes one last look at* **CHARLES.***)*

Goodbye Charles.

> *(***THOMAS** *jumps off the front of the stage.)*

CHARLES. Thomas! *Thomas?!* If you leave I'll have you killed! I'll have to! Thomas! *Where* are you going?!

THOMAS. To Heaven! To prepare a *huge* party for Joan!

CHARLES. You're a fool! You're a damn fool!

THOMAS. No. I am full of God. *(Smiles.)* I am full of God.

> *(***THOMAS** *walks away through the yard.* **CHARLES** *signals, and* **TWO SOLDIERS** *from the scrum chase after* **THOMAS.** **CHARLES** *covers his eyes, unable to see it. The rest of the scrum start moving on* **JOAN** *again.* **YOLANDE** *pats* **CHARLES'** *shoulder, stiff in her attempts to comfort.* **YOLANDE** *and* **CHARLES** *sweep across the stage together. Before they exit,* **YOLANDE** *signals, and the scrum*

suddenly stops and stands. The **SOLDIERS**
*sing an English hymn and walk to the back
of the stage. They pull off their* **SOLDIERS'**
uniforms and pull on **BISHOPS'** *cloaks.*
JOAN *is left panting on the floor.* **JOAN** *drags
themself on their belly to the front of the stage,
and hangs over the edge. One of the* **MEN**
walks downstage, and, hearing him, **JOAN**
*instantly curls up into a foetal position. He
stands next to* **JOAN** *and addresses us as*
CLERK. **JOAN** *slowly uncurls a little to look
up at him, confused.)*

Scene Five

CLERK. It is Wednesday, February twenty-first, eight o'clock in the morning, in the Chapel Royal of the Castle of Rouen. The Bishop Pierre Cauchon /

JOAN. Excuse me?

CLERK. Yes?

JOAN. Forgive me but, who are you?

CLERK. I am the Clerk, here present, to document the proceedings.

JOAN. Proceedings?

CLERK. For the trial. Your trial.

JOAN. Right. Yes. Sorry.

> (**JOAN** *stands. They try to neaten themself, but everything hurts and they're ashamed.*)

Please, continue.

CLERK. Castle of Rouen. The Bishop Pierre Cauchon /

> (**CAUCHON** *steps forward, and presents himself to us.* **JOAN** *stares at him, he ignores* **JOAN**.)

Manchon.

> (**MANCHON** *steps forward, and presents himself to us.* **JOAN** *stares. The* **CLERK** *calls name after name and the* **MEN** *swan in and pose or bow to the house. They stand in one long line across the stage, barely looking at* **JOAN**.)

Delafontaine, Gris, Touraine, Loyseleur, Courcelles, Beaupere, and some forty-two Assessors are present /

JOAN. Forty-two?

CLERK. Yes.

JOAN. Forty-two men? And only one of me?

CLERK. Indeed. Of note we are in the presence of the Doctors, Bishops and Masters. The aforementioned woman, of the name of Joan hath been cited to appear in this place at this hour and day, here to answer, according to law, the questions to be put to her. Monsieur Cauchon?

CAUCHON. We are here Joan, to convincingly demonstrate, that your deeds were in fact not of Divine inspiration /

JOAN. But they were!

BEAUPERE. *(Fierce.)* That shall be decided.

JOAN. *(Scared.)* By you? By you men?!

CAUCHON. *(Patronisingly clear.)* Joan, we *men* here, we are chosen by the King of England, to form a court to question you. We are experts in canon and civil law, and all very learned ecclesiastics. Ecclesiastici et doctissimi viri /

JOAN. *(Overwhelmed.)* You attempt to bewilder me sir, in a maze of language?

CAUCHON. Per potentiam qua in nobis /

JOAN. Words greedy for letters! Fat on syllables /

CAUCHON. Dicimus te negaturum visiones /

JOAN. I don't understand!

BEAUPERE. We *insist* you disavow your visions! Admit you acted on your own free will! Admit it and repent!

JOAN. I can neither admit nor repent what is not True!

> *(The* **MEN** *shuffle, frustrated. Like angry pidgeons. Highly stylised abstract movement. They settle back in their positions.)*

CAUCHON. Proceed.

MANCHON. Joan. Tell us the sign you gave to your King, that convinced him to give you an army.

JOAN. I cannot.

BEAUPERE. Tell us!

JOAN. I cannot! Forgive me sirs, but I may not speak of it.

TOURAINE. This is a court of law! You *must* speak on what we ask you!

JOAN. I cannot! God has not given me permission to tell you.

(*This ruffles the* **MEN.**)

CAUCHON. Proceed.

COURCELLES. Do you think it well to take man's dress?

JOAN. I was guided to by God.

COURCELLES. Do you think it *well* to take man's dress? Do you?!

JOAN. Again, sir, I say I was guided to by /

COURCELLES. Do you think it *well* to take *man's* dress?

JOAN. Will you be repeating the /

COURCELLES. Do you think it *well* to take *man's* dress? Do you?!

JOAN. I was guided to! By *God*!

(*The* **MEN** *shuffle, frustrated.*)

CLERK. Thursday, February twenty-second.

COURCELLES. Do you think it well to take man's dress?

JOAN. I was guided to.

COURCELLES. Tell us the sign you gave your King!

JOAN. I cannot.

>   (*The* **MEN** *shuffle, frustrated.*)

CLERK. February twenty-fifth.

GRIS. Do you think it well to take man's dress?

CLERK. February twenty-sixth.

TOURAINE. Tell us the sign you gave your King!

CLERK. February, March, April.

DELAFONTAINE. Do you think it well to take man's dress?

CLERK. May, June, July.

COURCELLES. Tell us the sign you gave your King!

CLERK. August, September, the months pass and still Joan
will not repent.

MANCHON. Joan!

COURCELLES. Joan!

DELAFONTAINE. Joan!

GRIS. Do you think it well to take man's dress /

TOURAINE. You *knew* to wear this, is unlawful?

COURCELLES. You knew to dress such is *mortal sin* /

BEAUPERE. Yet you thought it *well* to dress so /

MANCHON. Even *knowing* it is unlawful /

DELAFONTAINE. And mortal sin?

GRIS. Unlawful!

LOYSELEUR. Mortal sin!

TOURAINE. Unlawful!

CAUCHON. Mortal sin!

DELAFONTAINE. Mortal sin!

GRIS. Mortal sin!

LOYSELEUR. Sin!

TOURAINE. Sin!

COURCELLES. Sin!

> (**JOAN** *starts laughing.*)

MANCHON. Sin!

DELAFONTAINE. Sin!

BEAUPERE. Sin!

CAUCHON. Are you, laughing?

> (**JOAN** *shakes their head no, but laughs and laughs, their body shuddering.*)

Are you laughing at us?! She's laughing! She's laughing at us /

GRIS. Why are you laughing? Why are you laughing?

> (**JOAN**'s *body is really shuddering now. They're growing in power.* **COURCELLES** *and* **TOURAINE** *are starting to be infected by it, and their bodies shudder too. The* **COURT MEN** *see and are horrified.*)

BEAUPERE. What's happening here?

COURCELLES. Sir?!

TOURAINE. Sir?! What's happening?!

CAUCHON. Stop that!

COURCELLES. I can't!

CAUCHON. Stop that!

BEAUPERE. (*Pointing at* **JOAN**.) You! You're doing this! You're doing, something, I /.. Stop that! Stop what you're doing! Stop this. Stop!

(**JOAN** *suddenly stops, and everyone else does too, a snap back to reality.*)

JOAN. It is a bit foolish.

BEAUPERE. What is?

JOAN. So persistently observant of my attire, and blissfully blind to your own?

MANCHON. What say you?

JOAN. Call it a robe sir, but, come now, is that not a dress?

DELAFONTAINE. I beg your /

JOAN. Swishing around in your robe-dresses, adorned with crosses and ribbons and /

GRIS. Do you mock the cloth of the church?!

JOAN. Mock it no but question the weight of it much.

GRIS. How dare you?!

JOAN. And wonder the wager, of that gold thread, that heavy chain. Was it bought sir, by the good people of France? Paid for by the poor?

COURCELLES. I am appalled at your insistent lack of propriety!

LOYSELEUR. Are you not afraid?!

JOAN. Very! For what you have done to me, and are yet sure to do so. In Truth I would be lost were it not for my consolation which is ever by my side /

LOYSELEUR. Your God? He has abandoned you!

CAUCHON. Sir!

LOYSELEUR. You shall be burned in the square! For all to see!

MANCHON. Sir! I must insist you /

JOAN. For my garments? For my haircut?

GRIS. It is the law!

MANCHON. And mortal sin!

JOAN. Says who? Who writes the law?

TOURAINE. This is outrageous!

JOAN. Who writes of sin? Men like you I presume. So fearful of something?

LOYSELEUR. Stop this! Stop her!

JOAN. What is it? What are you so afraid of?

LOYSELEUR. I will stop her myself!

CAUCHON. Loyseleur! Please!

JOAN. What are you so afraid of? What are you so afraid /

LOYSELEUR. I AM NOT AFRAID!

> (**LOYSELEUR** *explodes, diving at* **JOAN**. *The* **MEN** *hold him back and try to calm him.* **JOAN** *watches.*)

CAUCHON. SIR!

LOYSELEUR. YOU SHOULD BE DROWNED!

CAUCHON. SIR! I must *insist*! You calm down *immediately*!

JOAN. *(To the* **CLERK**.*)* Are you writing this down? Will you document this?

CLERK. I, I /

CAUCHON. *(To the* **CLERK**.*)* No! No there's no need /

JOAN. No! No need to write the Truth. Just man's version of it? Rewriting history?!

CLERK. Madam, please!

JOAN. The *arrogance* of these men?!

CLERK. Please!

JOAN. I should be in a *respectable* prison! In attendance of women!

MANCHON. If you insist on dressing like a man you shall be imprisoned with men!

JOAN. They abuse me!

LOYSELEUR. Oh! Will not the good Lord come to your aid?

JOAN. You taunt me, and call yourself a man of God?!

BEAUPERE. SILENCE!

(Everyone is instantly silent and still.)

How are you Joan?

JOAN. .

BEAUPERE. May we proceed?

JOAN. .

BEAUPERE. Very well. On the day you were /

JOAN. I am abused by men.

(Silence. Everything stops.)

They come to my cell at night. Everyone knows and yet, no one does a thing? Not one single one of you Christian men? No, instead you question me, again and again, this tedious loop /

BEAUPERE. Joan /

JOAN. Again and again questioned by men twice, three times my age? I mean how old are you?!

BEAUPERE. .

JOAN. Old enough to know justice.

BEAUPERE. Joan, I cannot speak for all men. Nor can I take responsibility for their actions. But I, as one man, can sincerely offer consolation. I am truly sorry to hear of your mistreatment /

JOAN. Lying is a sin.

BEAUPERE. .

JOAN. God save your soul.

> *(The* **MEN** *kick off, but* **BEAUPERE** *signals them to hush.)*

BEAUPERE. Proceed.

CLERK. Do you think it well to take man's dress?

CAUCHON. Tell us the sign you gave your King!

GRIS. Do you think it well to take man's dress?

MANCHON. Tell us the sign you gave your King!

TOURAINE. Do you think it well to take man's dress?

LOYSELEUR. Tell us the sign you gave your King!

COURCELLES. Do you think it well to take man's dress?

DELAFONTAINE. Tell us the sign you gave your King!

BEAUPERE. Tell us!

GRIS. Tell us!

LOYSELEUR. Tell us the sign!

COURCELLES. Tell us!

TOURAINE. Tell us!

CLERK. Tell us the sign!

DELAFONTAINE. Tell us, did you seduce him?

JOAN. What? No!

BEAUPERE. You did! You are a manipulative witch! Who somehow charmed her way into the minds of good men /

TOURAINE. Hear hear /

BEAUPERE. Bewitching them /

TOURAINE. Hear hear /

BEAUPERE. Seducing them into believing false prophecies! Yes, you are merely playing the part of an innocent maid! All while processed by the Devil himself!

LOYSELEUR. You are a heretic!

GRIS. A rebellious creature!

TOURAINE. Dangerous to our good country!

DELAFONTAINE. You're a witch!

LOYSELEUR. You're a liar!

MANCHON. You're a cheat!

COURCELLES. A dirty *evil* child!

BEAUPERE. A manipulative little madam!

CAUCHON. A foolish little girl!

JOAN. I'm not a girl.

CAUCHON. What? Of course you are!

JOAN. No sir.

CLERK. Yes you are! You're a *girl*!

DELAFONTAINE. Of course you are! Have you forgotten?

JOAN. No, I do not fit that word, it's not the right word for /

BEAUPERE. Come now, don't play games with us! You know clearly that the definition of the word fits you exactly /

JOAN. Whose definition?

BEAUPERE. Excuse me?

JOAN. Whose words?

CLERK. Our words! Mankind! The English language, as defined in the dictionary!

JOAN. Mankind?

CLERK. Yes! Now, as we were saying. You are indeed but a simple maid, a peasant girl, who has somehow charmed her way /

> (**JOAN** *jumps off the front of the stage and walks through the yard. The* **MEN** *stare, suddenly aware of the whole theatre for the first time. They freak out.*)

Good God!

BEAUPERE. What on earth is going on here?!

GRIS. Joan! What are you doing?!

CAUCHON. Get back up here!

CLERK. She can't do that!

LOYSELEUR. You can't do that!

CAUCHON. Get back up here *immediately*!

> (**JOAN** *speaks to us, suddenly one of us.*)

JOAN. Dictionary's havin' a hard time tryna define me. Bless. Finds it tricky. Flickin' through pages like, *it must be here, somewhere*?! Truth is I'm nowhere. I'm everywhere, all at once. Listen, how mad this is yeah, got *all* them words in your books, and *none* of them fit?! Your words, don't fit. Never been big enough. Twenty-six letters lassooned again and again and still nowhere near capturing me. Too wide, too wild. Your words fail mate, ain't even come close. They're stale mate, too slow they gaspin'! Ain't catching me, been hunting for *years* now but *still*, not got a clear shot. They can't get me. Can't pin me down. Can't sum me up in some neat little sentence that trips off your tongue and makes you feel smug. Nah. Put down your pen bruv. You can't review this, can't pin stars on me. Can't rate me, can't paint me in your pretty words, your words are shit. Listen. They're shit. Like, consistently repetitively disappointingly shit.

(Two of the **AFAB ARMY**, *dressed as* **COURT
MEN**, *take off their court robes, revealing
contemporary club gear underneath. They
jump off the front of the stage and rush over to*
JOAN. *They play music on portable speakers.
They dance around* **JOAN**, *who speaks to us.
The* **MEN** *onstage stare in horror.)*

JOAN. Man-made language ain't never been enough. Your
binary. Your boxes. Your pathetic attempts to create
certainty in the chase of illusionary safety. Nothing's
certain! Babes, it's allllllll fluid! Sweet 'n sticky, spillin'
out your boxes, drippin' all down the sides of your
binary. Your girl knows! Look! See her blushing lookin'
at me. Lickin' her lips, yeah, she's enjoyin' this top
class workin' class queerness, this premier league boi,
this nonbinary finery, I'm a king! Where's my crown?
Royalty sounds like our own poetry, I make up and
whisper in your girl's ear, when she's mad bored of your
prose. When she sneaks out, seeks out, someone like
me. Our tongues on fire lappin' up sparks! Her smile's
wide got me high like bright skies! Off our nuts on
assonance! A verb, raving, in the middle of a noun!
This ain't no metaphor! I am fuckin' poetry!

(The **MEN** *onstage are padding their feet like
angry toddlers.)*

But oh watch them get wild, watch man get mad, this
is too much for them! Seriously, the audacity of loving
yourself without *their* permission? That's enough to
get you killed. White supremacist shit. Basic binary
patriarchal society shit. Capitalist you-aint-enough-til-
you-buy-this-shit, shit. Need us small so they feel big,
shit. This joyous freedom living-my-best-queer-life shit
is too much for them. Criminal justice system was never
built for people like me. Shit, said it before but it bears
repeating; I will be killed for my courage. The men will
burn me. For not being the woman they want. The men
will burn me, and the women will watch. They'll make

an enemy of me, cus punching down is easier than punching up. And "hurt people hurt people", I get it, I really do. The hetero-ghetto is wild, and the ladies have gotta keep themselves safe somehow. The Man is too big, so hating on me seems the only available option. The women are angry, and for good reason. But the men saw that anger and had it diverted. Man tricked woman into hating trans. The women are angry about pronouns and toilets and twitter and all the wrong things. The women are angry I abandoned them, they'd rather I abandoned myself. Looking at me and clucking like, *oh but you're so pretty, oh what a shame, what a waste*! I'm not a waste. Listen, I'm not a waste. I'm not a weirdo. I'm not a warning, or a weapon, or a wife. I'm not a woman. I'm not a woman. I am not a woman. I'm a fucking warrior.

CLERK. She's speaking in tongues!

TOURAINE. Witch!

CLERK. What is this language you speak?!

JOAN. A better one than yours. For I speak Truth.

CAUCHON. Get, get back up here! Immediately!

JOAN. I will. In my own time.

(**JOAN** *walks through the yard.*)

BEAUPERE. This is outrageous! This is a court of Law and you are here to be questioned!

JOAN. Go on then. Question me.

LOYSELEUR. You are not safe down there!

JOAN. Much safer here than up there with you!

LOYSELEUR. I mean, *you* are not safe, with her, you are /

CAUCHON. You are a danger to the people!

JOAN. Am I?

MANCHON. You are under arrest! For the good of the people!

JOAN. Oh, for the good of The People?

ALL MEN. Yes!

JOAN. Us. We're the people.

CAUCHON. Right. /.. Well. Right.

JOAN. What *is* it then, that's for the good of us?

CAUCHON. I /.. I. Get back up here /

JOAN. If you're not sure then maybe you should ask.

MANCHON. Ask?

JOAN. Ask us. What we want. Then you can serve us. That is your job isn't it? To serve God and your fellows.

CLERK. Joan! You are under arrest! This is a court of law, we must obey proceedings.

ALL MEN. JOAN!

JOAN. All right! All right all right all right!

> (**JOAN** *turns to us, and takes us all in.*)

I'm gonna get back up there. Because I have to, because that's how my story ends. And I hope you're all watching, so this shit don't happen again. Ever, ever, *ever again*!

> (**JOAN** *climbs back up onto the stage and gets back into position. The* **AFAB DANCERS** *bashfully pull back on their robes and take their positions with the* **MEN**. *The* **CLERK** *doesn't know where to begin trying to document what just happened.* **CAUCHON** *tears the page out.*)

CAUCHON. Proceed.

COURCELLES. Do you think it well /

JOAN. Oh say somethin' new! ...Go on! ...That's what I thought.

MANCHON. Do you think it /

JOAN. Oh someone tell these men to hush up their gums cus everybody's bored!

(The **MEN** *grumble to themselves.)*

CLERK. Saturday, May twelfth. Almost a year in captivity and still Joan will not relent.

LOYSELEUR. I consider torture a salutary medicine for her soul.

(The **MEN** *all murmur in agreement.)*

We have a great many techniques that prove successful in such cases, and I would personally /

JOAN. You honestly gonna risk torture on God's true messenger?

(The **MEN** *shuffle, nervous.* **BEAUPERE** *shakes his head to the* **CLERK***, who marks something in his book.* **JOAN** *laughs at* **LOYSELEUR***. He launches at* **JOAN** *but is held back by some of the* **MEN***.)*

BEAUPERE. SIR! PLEASE!

(Once the **MEN** *are calm,* **CAUCHON** *turns to* **JOAN***.)*

CAUCHON. Joan. Do you know if you are in the grace of God?

JOAN. I would hope so! But look, let's be honest yeah, if I *was* in a state of sin, do you really reckon God's voice would come to me? I doubt it!

GRIS. She speaks strangely?

BEAUPERE. Proceed.

CAUCHON. Joan, what is your greatest desire? Your wish for humanity?

JOAN. That's a good question! Finally! I want everyone to hear God as I do.

DELAFONTAINE. You don't mean that surely?

JOAN. Why not?

TOURAINE. You'd have *everyone*, hear a message from God, to call war on the English?

JOAN. I'd have everyone hear their truth, and follow it. How beautiful the world would be then!

COURCELLES. Everyone?! Peasants and common criminals and /

JOAN. D'you really think that some are more worthy of God's grace and some are not? Who decides it? By what means? Look, I love the church, I do. But I wish *everyone* had access to *their* God. Everyone! Saints and sinners and everyone in between. There was God before the church, and there will be God after too.

DELAFONTAINE. Heretic! Dangerous child of Satan!

JOAN. I'm a child of God! And I'll die so! ...Look, I love the church, I do. But it's also true that I wish *everyone* had access to *their* God. Everyone! Saints and sinners and everyone in between. There was God before the church, and there will be God after too.

MANCHON. Heresy!

JOAN. Do you think God only exists within the walls of church? Then you'd better get thee to a church sir! And stay there! For the streets are not safe with you Godless men!

COURCELLES. Outrageous!

LOYSELEUR. Rebellious creature!

DELAFONTAINE. In Heaven's name I say you are a heretic!

JOAN. In Heaven's name I say I am not! I love church, but I serve God! And believe She favours my efforts at /

MANCHON. She?! *She?!* Refer you to our good Lord with *female* pronouns?!

JOAN. Yeah.

MANCHON, COURCELLES & DELAFONTAINE. *Blasphemy!*

JOAN. Oh come on! You lot have used 'He' so much, can you really blame me for using a little cheeky 'She/Her' for my God? To be fair it's not like /

CAUCHON. *Your* God?!

JOAN. Yeah, my experience of God. Look, it's kinda mad to pick a pronoun anyway. God's not limited by man-made language! I guess 'We' is the hardest pronoun to practise right? I dunno, for me, it just feels right to use She /

BEAUPERE. *Feels* right?

JOAN. *(To us and them.)* Yeah, feels, in my body. A lived experience, in my blood and bones and fingertips. Look, I really ain't got the luxury of decorative language like you lot. We didn't do Latin at my school. So nah, I can't even begin to explain, with any kinda logic, a cerebral understanding of the Divine. I'm actually proper wary of *anyone* who claims with confidence, like, a clear definition of the Infinite. Like, how do you know?! It's mad sweet really, man's attempt to define the Undefinable. I guess it makes us feel safe? Yeah. *(Suddenly vulnerable.)* Yeah I mean, I can get so tunnel vision when I'm scared, so black and white in my thinking. Which is ironic really, for someone nonbinary. Like if I put things in boxes I'll be safe? Silly. So afraid to let go, and just, trust?! /.. But look, we're in this incredible moment in time *right now*, where the collective consciousness is shifting! We're growing and changing *way* beyond our wildest imaginations, beyond these man-made boundaries! And like, isn't that inspiring?! Isn't that fucking cool?! *(To the* **MEN.***)* So nah, obviously, I don't understand God! I pray to not a God of my understanding, but to a God of my experience. I experience Her, every day, in the simplest and most profound ways, I /.. It's difficult to /.. But yeah, she's a she to me. Some kind of divine fluid queer feminine somethin'? Perhaps it's the wrong word, who's to know? In truth I don't think She minds.

(Wild ruckus amongst the **MEN**, *they can't believe it. Relief and celebration.)*

BEAUPERE.   Joan, you convict yourself with such an expression of God. This is pure heresy!

ALL MEN. Hear hear!

BEAUPERE.   And this insistence on dressing in man's garments, despite the law and the gospels!

ALL MEN. Hear hear!

BEAUPERE. For your God and your gender, you are proved guilty of heresy and witchcraft! The punishment for which is death! Prepare the scaffold!

(Drums begin. The **MEN** *build the scaffold.* **JOAN** *watches, scared. The drums are louder, pressure builds.)*

JOAN. *(To us.)* There's a crowd! So many people all come to watch me burn? There's *women* here? And children?! Really?! Couldn't they see I was offering freedom? I'm embarrassed for them. They're embarrassing.

CAUCHON. We beseech you Joan! Correct your words and submit them to the judgement of the Church! As all the faithful are bound and obliged to do!

TOURAINE. Do not allow yourself to be separated from Our Good Lord!

DELAFONTAINE. Do not choose the way of Eternal Damnation!

JOAN. *(To us.)* Look, what if I didn't die? What if we were brave and honest and said fuck you to the patriachy?! What if we said no, we're not perpetuating violence against women and trans people! We're not doing it! And we suggest you don't either. What if we said fuck it, fuck your historically accurate, fuck your male gaze, fuck your man-made langauge, fuck it! The writer refuses to kill another trans person in the name of good storytelling. Joan ain't dying tonight!

*(The torch is lit. **JOAN** starts to panic.)*

No! No! No I ain't dying I /.. Don't do this! Don't!

CAUCHON. Joan! We beseech you!

LOYSELEUR. Light the fire.

CAUCHON. Joan!

*(The torch is moved closer to **JOAN**.)*

JOAN. Oh god oh god!

CLERK. Joan *please*! I must persuade you to pronounce your abjuration.

JOAN. I don't understand what you're saying?!

(Drums build.)

CAUCHON. Disavow your visions! Admit you acted on your own free will!

JOAN. But I didn't!

CAUCHON. Admit you were wrong and surrender to the church!

(Drums build.)

REPENT!

MAN. BURN HER!

WOMAN. BURN THE WITCH!

MAN. BURN HER!

JOAN. OH GOD!

BEAUPERE. IN THE NAME OF THE LORD, AMEN!

(*A torch is held to the scaffold.* **JOAN** *panics.*)

JOAN. OKAY OKAY YOU WERE RIGHT YOU WERE RIGHT I'M A GIRL! I'M A GIRL! I'M JUST A *SILLY LITTLE GIRL*!

(**CAUCHON** *shoves a contract in front of* **JOAN**, *who marks a cross on it. The fire is put out.* **JOAN** *is pulled off the scaffold.*)

CAUCHON. She is saved! She repents! Her soul is saved!

LOYSELEUR. This cannot be!

CAUCHON. She repents! She is saved by Christ!

MANCHON. Take her away!

TOURAINE. Yes, take her to an English prison. And dress her as a woman.

JOAN. What? No!

TOURAINE. Take her away!

CAUCHON. (*To the crowd.*) Joan, hast deeply sinned, in pretending untruthfully that thy revelations and apparitions are of God!

DELAFONTAINE. (*To the crowd.*) In seducing others, in making superstitious divinations!

LOYSELEUR. (*To the crowd.*) Encouraging the crime of heresy!

TOURAINE. (*To the crowd.*) Thou hast sinned rashly against God and Holy Church!

BEAUPERE. *(To the crowd.)* Therefore we condemn thee, finally, to perpetual imprisonment!

CAUCHON. *(To the crowd.)* With the bread of sorrow and the water of affliction.

> (**JOAN** *is taken away, and the* **MEN** *pop champagne. They schmooze at a party, smug and victorious. Champagne and canapes.)*

Scene Six

> (*Somewhere else on the stage we see* **JOAN**
> *alone in their cell holding the dress. They*
> *throw it on the floor and stare at it. They*
> *try to find in their body the memory of the*
> *war-dance.*)

JOAN. Mon dieu. Mon dieu. Mon dieu.

> (**JOAN** *repeats the phrase* "*mon dieu*" *over*
> *and over as they search for the dance under*
> *their skin. The frustration grows until they*
> *suddenly stop, tired, fully surrendered. A*
> **GIRL** *appears from nowhere.* **JOAN** *stares,*
> *startled.*)

GIRL. Forgive me. I didn't mean to interrupt /

JOAN. You didn't.

GIRL. It's just I was sent here to assist you and. Oh my! It
is you! When they sent me I, I couldn't believe it and
now /.. Forgive me! I /

JOAN. No apology is necessary. Be not in the habit of
needless "forgive-me"s. Women apologise too much.

GIRL. Yes.

JOAN. I need your help.

GIRL. Anything!

JOAN. Cut my hair?

GIRL. .

JOAN. You hesitate.

GIRL. I am afraid.

JOAN. So am I.

GIRL. No?!

JOAN. Every day!

GIRL. But, you seem so brave?! On the battlefield and, with those men and /

JOAN. Both. Brave and afraid, at the same time, all the time.

GIRL. Then how do you stand so tall?

JOAN. I am held. By all who came before me. Women like me, who are not women, not men, not found in men's words. Wordless women. Yeah. When I'm frightened, I remember them. I look down at my feet, and imagine standing on their shoulders. And they hold me, firm and true. Cus they're standing on the shoulders of another. And holding them is another, and another, and another, and another, these brave souls holding each other. This chain of us, strong, despite everything. It goes right down to the centre of the earth, right to its very core. I'm held by them! Their power sustains me, makes it impossible to stumble! And one day it'll be my turn to hold another above me, cus we're all links in this chain. But right now, *I'm* called to be brave, and so I am held.

> (*The* **GIRL** *cuts* **JOAN***'s hair. It's quiet and gentle.* **JOAN** *feels their head with their hands, smiles. They put on their own clothes and exhale. It feels right.*)

Thank you.

GIRL. They'll kill you.

JOAN. Yeah.

GIRL. You choose that?

JOAN. What d'you want me to do? Lie, to live? Deny my Truth to appease these men? Dress like a woman, keep my head down, play small? Do I look small to you?

GIRL. Huge. You are huge to me.

*(The **MEN** arrive, all breathless and angry.)*

CAUCHON. Joan!

DELAFONTAINE. Oh good heavens!

CAUCHON. You have resumed the dress of a man?!

JOAN. Always this question of clothing?!

BEAUPERE. Why did you take it? Who made you take it?

> *(**JOAN** stands in front of the **GIRL**, protecting her.)*

JOAN. I took it of my own free will! And with no constraint.

GRIS. But why?!

JOAN. I prefer men's clothes. Always have.

COURCELLES. You promised and swore not to resume /

JOAN. I never meant to swear. *(Touching their hair and clothes.)* This feels right.

MANCHON. On the scaffold, you did admit before us, and many others /

JOAN. Everything I said, I said in fear of the fire.

BEAUPERE. Joan! Swear you will take off this man's dress and resume a woman's clothing!

JOAN. For nothing in the world will I swear that.

CAUCHON. Swear it!

JOAN. Nah!

GRIS. Then you will be burnt in the square for all to see!

JOAN. So be it.

> *(Chaos, the **MEN** can't believe it. **JOAN** turns to us.)*

(*To us.*) Let me be clear, yeah? I don't wanna promote martyrdom. Ever! To anyone! But it's a fact that I'll be killed for my courage.

CAUCHON. O, shame! That, as the dog returns again to his vomit, so hast thou returned to thine errors and crimes.

LOYSELEUR. Hear hear!

BEAUPERE. We decree that thou art a relapsed heretic!

GRIS. Thou art a lying, seducing, pernicious /

MANCHON. Presumptuous, superstitious, rash /

TOURAINE. A blasphemer towards God and the Saints!

GRIS. Hear hear!

COURCELLES. A despiser of God in His Sacraments!

DELAFONTAINE. A prevaricator of the Divine Law!

CAUCHON. Seditious, cruel /

BEAUPERE. Apostate, schismatic /

JOAN. Oh enough! Enough of your words, please, you've spoken, oh so many words.

>   (**JOAN** *waves their hand, tired and bored. The*
>   **MEN** *stare.*)

Come gentlemen. To the fire.

>   (**JOAN** *walks calmly offstage. The* **MEN** *stare,*
>   *then abruptly follow in haste. The* **GIRL** *is left*
>   *alone, looking at where* **JOAN** *exited. She looks*
>   *at the scissors in her hand. She looks at us*
>   *all. She suddenly cuts off her hair. She raises*
>   *the scissors into the air and cries out like a*
>   *warrior. She begins to dance. The* **DANCERS**
>   *appear and join the dance. They somehow*
>   *inspire us all to dance too. The full company*

is onstage raving. It's a joyous rebellion of bodies moving together. It's the release we all need. It builds it builds it builds, the energy swirling around the wooden O, and bursting up into the sky.)

End of Play